The Sons of Ulster

The
SONS of
ULSTER

Ulstermen at War
from the Somme to Korea

RICHARD DOHERTY

Appletree Press

For my mother
ANNA
and all the womenfolk who waited, and prayed.
SPECTAMUR AGENDO

Published and printed by
The Appletree Press Ltd
19–21 Alfred Street
Belfast BT2 8DL
1992

This book has received support from the
Cultural Traditions Programme of the Community
Relations Council, which aims to encourage
acceptance and understanding of cultural diversity.

British Library Cataloguing-in-Publication Data
A catalogue record for this book is
available from the British Library.

ISBN 0 86281 342 5

9 8 7 6 5 4 3 2 1

Contents

Acknowledgements   7

Introduction   9

1   The Great War   11

2   Dunkirk, 1940   33

3   The Desert War   51

4   Italy   66

5   North-West Europe, 1944–45   83

6   Burma   97

7   War at Sea   112

8   War in the Skies   124

9   Prisoners of War   138

10 Korea   149

Conclusion   162

Bibliography   164

Picture Acknowledgements   166

Acknowledgements

The production of the radio programmes upon which this book is based, and the book itself, was greatly helped by a number of individuals and organisations, and that assistance is gratefully acknowledged.

The individuals include Colonel Robin Charley, OBE, formerly Curator of the Royal Ulster Rifles Museum, who provided many contacts, arranged a number of meetings and allowed the use of his office for interviews. Major Mike Murphy, his successor, gave access to photographs of 1st Royal Ulster Rifles in the Korean War.

Ernie Cromie, Chairman of the Ulster Aviation Society, was responsible for introductions to members of the Air Crew Association which provided the basis of the programme on the air war. Likewise, Ernie also assisted with the photographs for that chapter.

Ivan Glendinning of the Limavady Branch of the Royal British Legion was another who provided introductions. Regrettably, two men who assisted in arranging interviews died shortly afterwards: Bertie Cuthbert, Secretary of the Londonderry Branch, Royal Artillery Association, and Tommy McDonald, Secretary of 6 Light Anti-Aircraft Battery Association. Thanks are also due to John Ormsby and Colonel Harry Porter for their assistance, to Raymond Logue for arranging an interview with his late father, John Logue, and for photographs of his father.

Needless to say, all those who were featured in the programmes are included in these acknowledgements as well as those who were interviewed but whose words were not heard on air; some of the latter are featured, however, in this book. Many of the photographs in this book are from the archives of the Imperial War Museum. Thanks are due to the museum, and especially to Mrs Hilary Roberts of the Department of Photographs, for permission to use such material, to Michael Willis, also of the Department of Photographs, for his help in the museum, and to Maurice Riley who took the time and trouble to assist me in my research at the museum.

Special thanks are due to Michael McGowan who produced the series for Radio Ulster. It was Michael's professional skill and patient, sympathetic treatment of a novice broadcaster which turned a basic idea into a highly successful series and an important contribution to historical records. Likewise, thanks are also due to the staff of Appletree Press, particularly Douglas Marshall, for their highly professional work on the book and for advice and guidance during its production.

Finally, it would be remiss of me not to acknowledge the patient support and encouragement of my wife, Carol, and my children. Without their tolerance this book would not have been possible.

Introduction

THE idea for this book came originally from Michael McGowan, who produced the Radio Ulster series of the same name. Before any of the programmes were broadcast, he suggested that I should consider writing a book based on the series; the positive reaction from the listening public confirmed that idea.

Central to the radio series was the desire to allow the ordinary man to tell his story of warfare. There was no intention of painting pictures of grand strategy or of looking at campaigns from the viewpoint of a general. This was to be, as one old soldier put it, 'the worm's eye view of war'. Over ten weeks Michael and I talked to a number of soldiers, airmen and sailors. Sometimes they felt that they had nothing worth talking about, that their experiences would be of interest to no one. When persuaded to talk, they told their stories in a captivating and enthralling manner, and their modesty added to the attraction of the radio programmes. Hopefully that honesty and modesty has come across faithfully onto the printed page.

With the help of veterans, this book looks at some of the most climactic happenings of this century. Men who survived the horrors of the Western Front in the First World War tell of what it was like to squelch through thigh-high mud, to see men drown in mud, to lose comrades in the bombardment of trenches and dugouts. The confusion of the retreat to, and evacuation from, Dunkirk is captured in the words of men of three Irish infantry battalions who fought their way back to safety in 1940, while the story of the Desert War is recounted by soldiers of the only Irish unit to serve in that war from beginning to end. Others tell of Italy, the liberation of Europe, the war in the Far East and the struggle against the U-boats in the Battle of the Atlantic. And there is the poignant story of a sailor whose experiences in the Mediterranean provide a chilling reminder of the horrors of war at sea. Prisoners of war remember life in captivity under German and Japanese guard. And finally, the first United Nations war, in Korea, is brought to life through the words of men who lost many of their comrades in that country.

There is a variety of experience within these pages that has rarely been included in one book before. Accounts of war tend to concentrate on infantry or tank battles; these accounts tend to be attractive, with the dash of armoured warfare and the close-quarter battles of the foot-soldier. But men such as anti-aircraft gunners and the drivers of amphibious vehicles also played an important part in the many campaigns of the Second World War. To many they lack the 'glamour' of their infantry or armoured colleagues, but this book tells their stories – and they experienced their share of danger and made their own special contributions.

None of the men to whom we talked would describe themselves as heroes; yet they did many heroic things. One veteran said that he and his comrades simply 'went where we were sent and did as we were bid'. Nor would any of them wish to glorify war. It is that type of attitude that permeates these pages and shone out from the radio series. These were men who saw nothing special about themselves, but talking with them, listening to them, and broadcasting and writing their stories has been a humbling experience. They created a chapter of this island's history of which we can all be proud, irrespective of political or religious differences, which simply did not exist on the battlefield. Nor did differences in social background matter either. The men who feature in these pages came from city street and country cottage; some had been regular servicemen in peacetime but most were volunteers. Again, this was a largely irrelevant distinction. Some of the memories in this book are from officers, but the majority are those of ordinary servicemen who are representative of the many volunteers from every corner of Ireland and who fought in the campaigns and battles of three wars covered by the book. Whether town dweller or country lad, volunteer or regular, officer or other rank, Catholic or Protestant, the sons of Ulster knew a comradeship and a trust in adversity that should be a lesson to us all.

Since the radio series was first broadcast a number of the men who were interviewed have died. In passing into history themselves, they remind us of the need to record the memories of the ordinary man so that a more complete picture of their times can be passed on to future generations.

Richard Doherty

1

The Great War

If you stand up you're shot and if you stoop down you're drowned.

T HE FIRST WORLD WAR, or the Great War as it was known until another even more terrible war followed it, began on 4 August 1914. Britain quickly sent an army, the British Expeditionary Force (BEF), to France to help the French and Belgians against German attacks. Most military historians agree that this was the best-prepared and best-trained British army to ever take the field at the beginning of a war. So speedy and efficient was its mobilisation, that the BEF was in place on the northern flank of the French army, facing the Belgian border, by 23 August. Its importance, however, was dismissed by the German High Command, who are alleged to have called it a 'contemptible little army', and hence the original members of the BEF were to become famous as the Old Contemptibles.

Many of those Old Contemptibles belonged to Irish regiments; among the BEF's Irish units was 2nd Battalion, Royal Inniskilling Fusiliers. Typical of the Skins who went to France with the BEF in August 1914 was **David McGinley**, who was wounded in action and invalided back to England. His injuries made him unfit for further active service in France. He was, however, capable of serving in a garrison battalion and thus found himself transferred to 1st Garrison Battalion, Royal Irish Fusiliers, in India, where he died of illness on 12 March 1916.

The Irish Guards were also in the BEF and were soon in action. At Ypres on 1 November 1914 they suffered no fewer than 350 casualties, among whom was **Guardsman John Ormsby**. He had been an Irish Guardsman before the war, but left the regiment to become a policeman in the Royal Irish Constabulary. When war broke out he returned to the Guards, and was one of many members of the RIC who served and died in that regiment. He has no known grave, but his name is inscribed on the Menin Gate at Ypres,

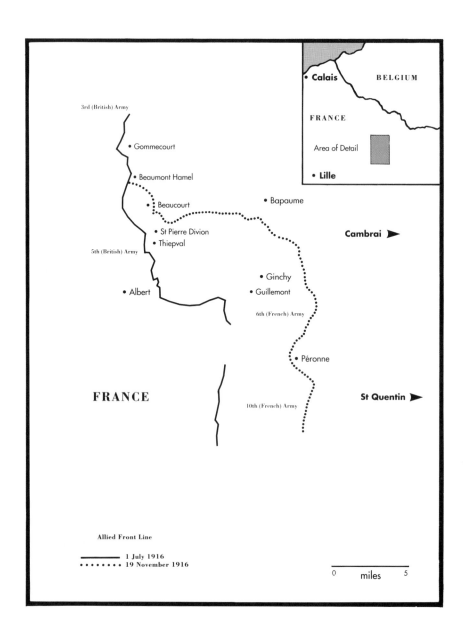

3rd (British) Army

• Gommecourt

• Beaumont Hamel

• Beaucourt

• St Pierre Divion

• Thiepval

5th (British) Army

• Bapaume

Cambrai ▶

• Ginchy

• Guillemont

6th (French) Army

• Albert

• Péronne

St Quentin ▶

FRANCE

10th (French) Army

Calais   BELGIUM

FRANCE

Area of Detail

• Lille

Allied Front Line

———— 1 July 1916
• • • • • • • 19 November 1916

0   miles   5

that moving tribute to the many British troops who fell in the Ypres sector and who have no known resting-place. Since 1919 the Last Post has been sounded and silence observed at 8.00 each evening at the gate in memory of those whom it honours.

The BEF had trained for a war of movement but found itself fighting a defensive battle against Von Kluck's army, which outnumbered it by more than three to one. At Mons the Germans were stopped by the British troops, but the number of Germans was overwhelming, and the British army, threatened with encirclement, was forced to fall back to the River Marne. The German armies had suffered so badly at the hands of their retreating opponents, however, that they could go no further and came to a halt on the Marne. Thus was Paris saved from the Germans in what was described at the time as 'the miracle of the Marne'.

From the line of the Marne the Allied armies launched a counter-attack, pushing the Germans back to the River Aisne where the situation settled down, principally because both armies were thoroughly exhausted. The opposing forces began to dig defensive positions; by the end of October 1914 the pattern of trench warfare on the Western Front was being established. It was to last until the spring of 1918, with the opposing trenches stretching from the sea to the Swiss frontier.

During 1915 the armies involved in the conflict learned the truth about trench warfare, and soldiers found out how to survive in horrific conditions. By that time, however, the original BEF with its regular soldiers had virtually ceased to exist. In its wake had come the armies formed from the Territorial Force, and then, by the end of the year, the first of Kitchener's new volunteer armies began to arrive in France. With the latter came 16th (Irish) and 36th (Ulster) Divisions. Both formations had been born out of the political turmoil of Ireland in the days before the war. Many men of 16th Division had been members of the nationalist Irish Volunteers, while most of 36th Division were members of the Ulster Volunteer Force, although some had joined up independently.

One such eager recruit was seventeen-year-old **Thomas Gibson** from Garvagh, who made his way to Coleraine to join 10th Royal Inniskilling Fusiliers – the Derry Volunteers. At Coleraine railway station he took his place in a queue, and when his turn came to face the recruiting sergeant he answered truthfully about his age:

> The sergeant told me to go away and come back again when I was eighteen, but I saw another queue and so I joined in with that. I

Wellington Barracks, London, 12 August 1914. Soldiers of the Irish Guards prepare to leave for France to join the British Expeditionary Force. By the end of the year most of the men in this photograph were dead or wounded.

decided that I wasn't going to tell the truth the second time. But before I came forward to the recruiting sergeant I saw a train about to pull out and a lot of me pals were on it . . . so I rushed over to the train and got in just as it was moving off. Well, it took me to Finner [Camp] where the Derry Skins were forming. I was there nearly a month in 15 Platoon of D Company before they discovered that I wasn't in the army at all, because I hadn't been sworn in.

The irregularity of young Gibson's position, along with that of several others, was soon put right, and the training routine of the battalion continued.

Londonderry city provided more than half the strength of 10th Inniskillings, with two companies being raised there. **Harry Bennett** was one of the Derry Volunteers and he recalled that several men came home to join the battalion. One of these was **Jimmy Porter**, who was quickly promoted to sergeant and who earned the nickname Fadeaway from his habit of dismissing squads with the words, 'Fade away, boys, fade away.' An older brother of Harry Bennett – Jack – came home on leave from the Indian civil service some time later, volunteered for war service and was subsequently commissioned into 10th Inniskillings.

In County Antrim the Volunteers were joining battalions of the Royal Irish Rifles, which also recruited in Belfast. Around Ballyclare most of the eligible young men joined up with C Company, 12th Royal Irish Rifles; this was to have a profound effect on Ballyclare less than two years later. However, **Bob Grange** found himself not in the infantry battalion, in which most of his friends enlisted, and which he wanted to join, but in the Divisional Signal Company of the Royal Engineers.

In July 1915 the Ulster Division moved to England to receive its artillery and undergo further training. Field Marshal Lord Kitchener inspected it on 20 July at Seaford, and in early September the division moved to Bordon and Bramshott where it was declared ready for service. Soon afterwards orders were issued for the division to move to France, and it was concentrated in the Amiens area by early October. Having moved much earlier than originally planned, the Ulstermen had gone without their own artillery; their gunners were temporarily replaced by London Territorials.

The Ulsters were soon introduced to the front line: 'Some time about the end of October we moved up and we went into the front line, and I was all surprised to find that we were just within a hundred yards of the German

'Some parts of the line were very bad.' An officer of 12th Royal Irish Rifles (centre) is one of three officers wading through the mud of a communication trench in 1917.

lines' (Thomas Gibson). At first it was fairly quiet in the line: 'It was rare to see anybody wounded even for the first fortnight, but that soon changed' (Harry Bennett). As one of Harry Bennett's first comrades to be seriously wounded was rushed past, Bennett heard him saying, 'What's my poor mother going to say about this?' The pathos of that moment struck Harry Bennett forcibly: 'It seemed so sad there. It was the first time it dawned on me, the seriousness of the war, I mean.'

Not everywhere was quiet, however.

> Some parts of the line were very bad, especially a place which we had taken from him . . . . The shellfire had smashed up all his trenches and we had to live in that. There was one particular place and we were in mud, walking about up to our knees nearly.
>
> *Thomas Gibson*

The normal spell of four days in the trenches saw men turn into living sculptures of mud, as they waded through the mire of the trenches, rubbing against the wet walls. Weapons became encrusted with slime while the cold of the winter presented further problems. To combat the cold, goatskin jerkins were issued but, according to Bob Grange, were soon discarded by many as the goatskin only seemed to provide a warm habitation for undesirable companions. Leather jerkins or greatcoats were later substituted.

In those early days in France Bob Grange found that his job was to be a signaller for the artillery's Forward Observation Officers (FOOs). This was as dangerous as being an infantryman, since it involved moving forward with attacking infantry to lay cables for the FOOs in order to direct the fire of the supporting guns.

The Ulster Division was introduced to action gradually, and its men were involved in night patrols which went out to raid the German lines. Often the object of such patrols was to bring back prisoners for questioning about the enemy's plans. Such raids were unpopular with the soldiers, as they frequently brought furious reaction from the German artillery with intensive bombardments, which the victims termed 'hates'. The division's first major action was the Battle of the Somme in July 1916, an offensive aimed at taking the pressure off the French at Verdun and at breaking through the German front line. At 7.30 am on 1 July 1916 the first wave of over 60,000 British soldiers attacked along an eighteen-mile front, on what was to become the most unforgettable day in the history of the Ulster Division.

The division was effectively only in the battle on that first day, during which it lost nearly 6,000 men – killed, wounded or missing. Bob Grange recalled the assault as the day when 'all my pals went down'. They were the men of the Ballyclare company – C Company, 12th Royal Irish Rifles – who were on the extreme left of the Ulster Division's sector that morning. To their left was 29th Division, which never got into the German front-line trench. Because 29th failed to achieve its objectives, the advancing Rifles had to suffer heavy German machine-gun fire from their left flank:

> Everytime they pushed forward they were enfiladed with the heavy machine-gun fire. C Company made three charges across no man's land that morning and of course got wiped out.
>
> *Bob Grange*

That July morning in 1916 over 20,000 troops were killed in one of the war's greatest tragedies. The regiment which suffered most was the Royal Inniskilling Fusiliers. One battalion of the Inniskillings was almost wiped out, and the regiment as a whole suffered 2,208 dead, the greatest death toll ever inflicted on a single regiment of the British Army in one day. The effect at home was devastating. **James Conaghan** was a fourteen-year-old living in the Waterside area of Londonderry. He was never able to forget the days following the attack on the Somme. Until his death he could recall quite clearly the arrival of the telegram messages in his neighbourhood. Hardly a house was spared. The womenfolk of the district were overwhelmed with grief as news came of the deaths of husbands, fathers, sons, brothers or boyfriends: 'The women were out in the streets, screaming and crying. Some homes had lost more than one man. It was . . . just terrible on them.' That particular area of the city included Ebrington Barracks. There were many army families living in the streets around the barracks, as well as families of men who had joined up from both the Irish and Ulster Volunteers. Now all were bound together in the communal tragedy.

There had been high hopes for the Somme offensive. The High Command had expected the attack to be, literally, a walkover and had ordered the soldiers to march across no man's land in parade-ground formation. Nevertheless, these high hopes were dashed as German machine-guns tore British battalions to

On the Somme. Supporting soldiers move up to the attack at Ginchy in September 1916.

shreds on that fine summer morning. Clearly, there were many reasons for the disaster. Bob Grange formed his own theory as to why so many were lost on the first day of the Somme battles:

> One of the chief reasons, I think, for what it's worth, was the effect of the French people. They asked Haig [the British commander-in-chief] to postpone his attack from dawn until 7.30 am, broad daylight, and the result was that the men had to go over in broad daylight against the German machine-gun fire and artillery, whereas if there'd been a dawn attack they'd have been half across no man's land . . . and saved all that carnage . . . . I think that was where the attack failed badly.

Not only has it been argued that the timing of the attack on the Somme was wrong, but that the plan was flawed from the start. That morning over 100,000 men had attacked in two waves along a front of eighteen miles, and the length of that front meant that the British artillery was spread too thinly to provide an effective bombardment. In addition, there were insufficient heavy guns. All of this was exacerbated by a high percentage of defective shells which failed to explode at all. The German troops were so well dug in that the British bombardment was little more than a nuisance, and the PBI, or the Poor Bloody Infantry as they called themselves, discovered just how ineffective the bombardment had been when German infantry climbed up from their dugouts to open fire with machine-guns as the British troops made their way across no man's land. In the midst of all this disarray, the Ulster Division achieved what some considered to be impossible:

> In between . . . Thiepval and Beaumont Hamel there was a terrific fort . . . dead in the centre called Schwaben Redoubt, and the Germans boasted that that couldn't be taken. And our own army command were of the opinion that it couldn't be taken by a frontal attack. The idea had been, I think, that they'd get round on its flanks and get it from the rear. But the whole thing went 'flop' and the two divisions on either side of us were blocked, and the place that couldn't be taken, we took it, our troops took it and went right through it and away up to the edge of Grandcourt, what was left of them that morning. That's about nearly three miles, and the Inniskillings were the people who got the furthest forward that morning as far as I can remember now.

Bob Grange

Both 9th (Tyrone Volunteers) and 10th (Derry Volunteers) Inniskillings were the units to which Bob Grange referred. Neither Harry Bennett nor Thomas Gibson had gone forward in the advance that morning. Thomas Gibson was ill in hospital while Harry Bennett, an orderly at battalion headquarters, had lost out in the draw to see who would join in the attack. Bennett remembers: 'I had wanted to go up but I didn't get going. I went as far forward as I could, but then we weren't allowed to go any further and had to go back and wait in the HQ.' As already noted, Bob Grange was a Ballyclare man and most of the young men in the town who were eligible to enlist did so. And like Londonderry, where James Conaghan had witnessed the grief of the news from the front, Ballyclare, too, was stunned at the reports from France:

> Ballyclare, that day . . . had over thirty killed and over a hundred wounded and, mind you, that was a packet for such a small place. I was about two years out when I got my first leave and when I came home they told me that for several weeks after the first of July, everytime they heard a knock at the door their hearts nearly stopped beating: 'Was it a telegram?'
>
> *Bob Grange*

It was difficult for people in Ballyclare, and elsewhere, to come to terms with the human tragedy of the Somme, but what of the soldiers who lived through that day? The full effect didn't occur until three or four months after the attack. This happened, perhaps, when a soldier was sitting alone and thinking about the war, and about the friends he would never see again. As Bob Grange recalled: 'That's when you felt it most. At the time, you see, with the excitement and the noise, you never gave it a thought.' Bob Grange's experience was one he knew he shared with many other survivors of that fateful day.

As the Ulster Division was withdrawn from the line, the battalions held roll-calls to assess their losses. In Martensart Wood, Harry Bennett was one of those who paraded in the ranks of 10th Inniskillings, now over 400 men fewer in number than they had been at 7.30 the previous morning. It was a poignant occasion which would remain with the survivors for the rest of their days.

Battle of Messines – the village of Wytschaete on 8 June 1917, the day after its
capture by 16th (Irish) and 36th (Ulster) Divisions. Nationalist MP Willie Redmond,
a major in the Royal Irish Regiment and younger brother of John Redmond, the
Nationalist Party leader, was wounded in the battle and rescued by stretcher-bearers
of the Ulster Division. Already fifty-seven, Redmond died from his wounds that
same day.

A name would be called and someone would answer, 'He's dead', then
another name and the same answer. One of the men who died was
Sergeant Porter, Fadeaway Porter, we called him. He was a great
bloke, very popular. I lost a lot of friends that day.

Harry Bennett

In his hospital bed Thomas Gibson was shocked to see the number of
casualties brought in and could hardly believe the suffering which his own
company had endured. For men who, by a stroke of fate, had survived that
day by not being in the attack, the shock of the loss of so many friends was
more immediate.

The battle on 1 July was not the only battle fought in 1916. The Somme
battles lasted from July until November, resulting in a German withdrawal
to the Hindenburg Line in February 1917, a year that was to see the first
major British success in the war with the Battle of Messines in June, a
well-planned, carefully rehearsed attack. The Ulster Division underwent
intensive training before the assault and then:

We were taken up the night before and we were standing in the
trench ready to go over when the mines went up, and that was one
of the largest mines they ever had in France. As soon as the mines
went up we went over the top and we went on and the whole place
was devastated.

Thomas Gibson

The explosion was a key part of the strategy to break the German lines at
Messines and had been carefully planned over several months. Tunnelling
companies of Royal Engineers – many of the sappers were miners in civilian
life – had laboured to dig their way under the German fortifications and
had placed 500 tons of high explosives in preparation for the attack. This
tunnelling sealed the fate of the German defences at Messines.

During the excavation work field-telephones were provided in each of the
tunnels, and Bob Grange, now a sergeant, was one of the signallers who
had the task of laying cables in a tunnel. This particular tunnel travelled
beneath the British front and second lines, across no man's land and beneath
the German line until it came to a 'huge concrete dugout'. This had been a
farmhouse at one time, but the Germans had turned it into an impressively

strong fortress. Whenever the tunnel got under Spanbroekmoelen – the fortified former farmhouse – it branched out into three separate chambers. High explosive mines were placed in each chamber, after which the charges were fused and set. The engineers sealed up the tunnels to create one massive landmine:

> And then up it went in the air at 3.10 am [on the morning of 7 June 1917] and they actually heard the explosion in England. It blew a hole . . . the size of a football pitch, about 120 yards . . . that was the width of the whole diameter of it. I was never as frightened in my life, the whole time I was out there. I've an idea now what people feel like in an earthquake. I was in the second line whenever it went up in the air and the ground moved. We were clawing the trench side to keep ourselves upright. There was a terrific flame and smoke and one thing and another went up into the air. And my officer that I had in the brigade I was with spoke German fluently and he interrogated several prisoners that day, and they told him that they'd had a big raiding party of almost 300 in Spanbroekmoelen and they intended to raid our lines to get prisoners at 6.00 in the morning. They were all packed into Spanbroekmoelen, getting ready for the raid, and unfortunately for them we started ours at 3.10 am, so they all went up in the air.
>
> I never saw a carnage like it in such a short space. There wasn't a human body [intact] lying round that place . . . just bits and pieces, arms, heads, feet, legs. Terrible mess.
>
> *Bob Grange*

The ground gained at Messines was captured largely by the efforts of 30,000 Irishmen of 16th Irish and 36th Ulster Divisions, with total losses of just over 2,000 dead, wounded or missing. The Germans had lost heavily. The German 2nd Division, which had been due for relief that night, had fewer than ten survivors, from a total of over 10,000 men. Overall, German casualties included some 20,000 dead.

By this stage in the war the face of the British Army had changed beyond all recognition through heavy losses. From the old Regular Army of 1914 to the Territorial Force and Kitchener's volunteer armies, it now came to be made up largely of hastily trained conscripts. And for the conscripts, as

Battle of Messines. German prisoners are escorted into captivity by soldiers of 16th (Irish) Division.

well as for the surviving regulars, it was impossible to relax at any time in the front-line trenches.

> [The trenches] were all smashed up and we were hanging out in dugouts, and we couldn't show ourselves in daylight because the Germans would have seen us, and all our work trying to fix up trenches was done at night. And I remember during that particular time the Germans were using a thing we called 'minnies'. They were about the size of oil tanks and they fired them across, and you could see them coming. There was a fellow and I used to watch for these coming and run up and down the trench to escape them, and there was a friend of mine from Garvagh and two others lying sleeping in one of the dugouts, and one of these 'minnies' just landed straight in the dugout. They were just blown into smithereens.
>
> *Thomas Gibson*

Even worse, the running had to be done in clinging mud, which could be more than ankle-deep.

Thomas Gibson escaped that night, but some months later at Cambrai he was wounded by German machine-gun fire and became the envy of his friends in the trenches:

> I was standing on the firestep, and my head was just above the parapet looking out across no man's land, and it was a moonlit night so that you could see well, and you had to be pretty well on your guard in case he would sneak up. And all of a sudden he opened up with a machine-gun . . . the first bullet hit the sandbag just to the right of my head, and it must have been an explosive bullet for it exploded and the small pieces all went into my head and through my ear and into my cheek. I thought at first, when he hit the sandbag, that a stone or something had hit me, and then the blood started to flow. I staggered into the next bay where the other fellow was on duty, and he called the stretcher-bearers and they bundled me up and I bled like mad. And I remember, when they were bringing me down the trench, some of the other boys were shouting, 'Boys, you're a lucky fellow, I wish it'd been me. You're the lucky boy getting away.'

What awaited Thomas Gibson was a comfortable hospital bed with regular hot meals, in stark contrast to the conditions which his friends had to put up with in the trenches. These conditions worsened when it was time for a frontal attack on the German lines:

> Before a push would start, in most cases you were put on hard biscuits and bully [beef] to allow all the transport to be diverted to bringing up all the supplies for the attack, so that you were on hard biscuits and bully for some time . . . . And then, of course, during the push you were lucky if you got any food at all other than that. You never saw hot food during an attack at all. In the infantry during an attack, nearly the most that the infantrymen would be in the front line, actually engaged in the battle, would be [for] about five days, sometimes three, but usually about five or six days and then they were drawn out, exhausted. But in the case of the artillery, once a push started we had to stay in right from the start until the finish, until you were pulled out.
>
> For instance, at the time of Messines, for the four weeks of that push, we were in there all that time and then we moved straight out of that up into Passchendaele, Ypres. We were in there for over eight weeks. There were three months [in which] we never had our clothes off. We never had our boots off all that time, no fresh clothing or anything. And we were saturated with the rain, plastered with the mud, a terrible time altogether.
>
> *Bob Grange*

According to one German general, Crown Prince Rupprecht, rain was the German army's most effective ally. Nowhere was this more true than at Ypres in 1917: 'The whole countryside was full of great, big shell holes, and they were full of water, and if you were passing along and fell into one of them you had a chance of being drowned before anyone could get you out' (Thomas Gibson).

> The day the push started, the rain started at about 8.00 that morning, and it got heavier and heavier until there was stairrods coming down. And it rained like that for six days and six nights without a break, and we were out in that the whole time, saturated to the skin. There were lots of them drowned in the mud that would have been saved under normal circumstances. I remember the morning that the 36th went over up at Ypres, the YCV Battalion – that was the 14th Rifles – had

Top: Relaxing after battle. Officers of a Royal Inniskilling Fusiliers battalion in 36th (Ulster) Division at Dranoutre with souvenirs of the Battle of Messines, 11 June 1917.

Left: Sergeant Thomas Robinson, who served in the Royal Inniskilling Fusiliers, the Royal Irish Regiment and the Worcestershire Regiment. Thomas Robinson had been active in the Boer War and wears the ribbon of the Queen's South Africa Medal. The cap-badge in this photograph is that of the Worcestershire Regiment.

to wade ankle-deep through water to get to the German front line. It was a terrible ordeal.

Bob Grange

Thank goodness we got out of that place. We were only in it about twelve days, but it was the worst place I had ever been in, the worst place any of us had ever been in. We were preparing for an advance there and I remember the morning of the advance. We had a new colonel at that time and we were going over at 8.30 in the morning, and he and his party of officers from the headquarters just happened to be at our bay whenever it came 8.30. And our barrage lifted, and when the barrage lifted that was the sign for us to get on the parapet and away. Now, these parapets were pretty high and slimey, and I was only a young fellow at that time and I was struggling to get up and put my rifle on the top . . . . And this big colonel, he just got me by the seat of the trousers and the back of the coat and he just shoved me onto the parapet and he said, 'Away you go, sonny.'

Thomas Gibson

At Ypres one of Harry Bennett's friends summed up the true horror of trench warfare in a sardonic remark that must be a classic piece of the black humour which flourishes among front-line soldiers. Herbie Andrews, 'a great joker', commented to Bennett shortly after their arrival in the sector: 'Harry, this is a terrible place they've took us . . . if you stand up you're shot and if you stoop down you're drowned.' It was small wonder that the Ypres sector, and especially Passchendaele, became a byword to describe the nature of the Western Front. The rain that was the Germans' greatest ally was, according to the Frenchman Henri Barbusse, 'hell' to the infantryman.

Yet, soldiers still tried to conceal the full horror of their conditions from their families at home. When front-line soldiers went home on leave they rarely discussed the mud and the blood of France. Harry Bennett was at home on leave at the same time as his battalion's chaplain. While walking with his mother one day the pair met the chaplain. Bennett was horrified when the clergyman began to regale his mother with graphic descriptions of the 'terrible place your son and his friends have to live'. The young soldier stood behind his shocked mother, gesticulating frantically at the chaplain in an effort to dissuade him from his subject, but to no avail.

In spite of the horrors to which they were subjected, front-line soldiers would still show remarkable examples of caring, not only for their own comrades but also, on occasion, for wounded opponents. At least once this gave rise to an unofficial truce, significantly at Ypres:

> All the time I was out, there was only once I saw a truce and that was up at Ypres. We'd been in supporting the 55th and then our own division, the 36th, and then the 41st Division after that, and each time those three divisions were decimated and had to be pulled out. The 41st Division got a terrible hammering, and all those men were lost trying to get one wee bit of a hill, 'Hill 35', they called it. And the 41st got such a bad drilling that they had a truce between themselves and the Germans and they crawled out on their hands and knees and started to bring in the wounded, and then further and further into no man's land, and the Germans, they didn't fire on them. And then the Germans, they did the same on their side, and then eventually they got up on their feet and they started to move forward and to bring the wounded in that way and eventually they started to fraternise and talk.
>
> One of the officers . . . ran back to divisional headquarters to see what was taking place. The GOC of the division sent a message through to the front-line troops to come back at once, for he was going to put a barrage down in no man's land in thirty minutes' time. I can always remember old Colonel Simpson, our colonel, giving the order to fire. But by that time they'd all got back in and the Germans had understood the message too and they only kept the barrage up for roughly three to five minutes, and then it died away again and it just went back into the lull that had developed after the fighting had ceased. It was a terrible day, that day.
>
> *Bob Grange*

The weakening of the British forces at Passchendaele at the end of 1917 inspired Ludendorff, the German commander, to attack the British armies in the area of Arras and St Quentin in the spring of 1918. It was there that 16th Irish Division was destroyed, but the British succeeded in withdrawing in spite of all their suffering and regrouped for the final Allied offensives. With the Americans now in the war, these offensives were to destroy the German army. In fact, the German High Command had suffered a devastating psychological blow when Ludendorff found that the British were able to counter-attack in the summer.

Gas Warfare

Poison gas, which killed many thousands on both sides, will be forever associated with the First World War. Gas was first used by the Germans against French, Algerian and Canadian troops in April 1915; early in May it was used against British troops.

Many died in the trenches into which the heavier-than-air gas fell – respirators were yet to be issued – in spite of their precautions. (A field dressing soaked in urine was a standard makeshift respirator.) Others survived for a time only to die later in agony. One man who died from gas poisoning after the war was **Sergeant Thomas Robinson**, who had joined the Royal Inniskilling Fusiliers in March 1882. Promoted to sergeant by 1886, he then fell foul of alcohol and dropped to corporal. By the beginning of the Boer War he was a sergeant again and served throughout the war, being wounded at the Battle of Colenso.

In 1914 Robinson was posted to the newly raised 6th Battalion of the Royal Irish Regiment, B Company, which consisted of Londonderry nationalist volunteers. After being gassed in France, he was transferred to the Worcestershire Regiment as an instructor. Invalided out of the army, Robinson died from the effects of gas on 29 March 1920, just over thirty-eight years after joining the army. One of the many victims of the Great War whose names are not found on any war memorial because death occurred after hostilities had ended, Thomas Robinson, at fifty-six, was certainly one of the oldest military victims of that war.

Before the German spring offensive of 1918 was launched, several battalions of 36th Ulster Division were disbanded, including 10th Inniskillings, some of whom went to 109 Trench Mortar Battery. Harry Bennett and **David Donaghy** found themselves in this unit, while **Jack Bennett** was an officer of the battery. As the division retreated, Jack Bennett saved the lives of several wounded men by swimming across a canal and pushing the injured on improvised rafts. Bennett was then wounded himself and was helped, at this stage, by David Donaghy, who brought him out of danger. For this action Donaghy was awarded the Military Medal, recommended by Jack Bennett: 'I was a bit surprised about that. They didn't tell me about it then. I got the medal later on.' Part of his surprise was due to the fact that he had carried out a similar rescue of a more senior officer before, during a night raid on the German lines. After dragging the wounded man by his belt out of no man's land, he did not even receive a word of thanks and did not expect one now. Bob Grange also finished the war with the Military Medal. Although he claimed 'it must have been a spare one they just gave to me', his medal was undoubtedly hard-earned in the dangerous life of a forward signaller.

The final months of the war saw a return to open warfare, as neither side had a chance to build up large trench systems. Fourth Ypres was a battle of movement as the Allies advanced for the last time. In October 1918, the Ulster Division was the first across the Lys near Courtrai, pushing the Germans further back until finally, with revolution breaking out at home, Germany sought an armistice; on the eleventh hour of the eleventh day of the eleventh month, the Great War – the 'war to end all wars' – came to an end with over ten million dead.

There are few Ulstermen alive today who came through the Great War. Bob Grange lived until he was ninety-six-years old and never forgot the time when he, as a young man, fought in those muddy plains of Flanders:

> It hits you in several ways, you know. It's something that, well, I'm glad that I went through because you learned an awful lot, what you would call self-sacrifice. You learned to think of your pal instead of yourself. And then there was the endurance of the human body, of what it can stand when it's pushed to the bit. You talk about these explorers in the Arctic and Antarctic and what they endure; well it's just the same when you're in battle there. Human life really means nothing at the tail end, except if it's your pal. Then you feel it.

2
Dunkirk, 1940

I wouldn't like to go to hell, and that's what it was.

WHEN ADOLF HITLER'S forces invaded Poland on Friday, 1 September 1939, Europe was plunged into war for the second time in twenty-five years. The British and French governments issued an ultimatum calling on Germany to withdraw from Poland. That call was ignored, and on Sunday morning, 3 September, Prime Minister Neville Chamberlain broadcast to the nation the news that the British government had declared war on Germany.

Once again a British Expeditionary Force was ordered to France. Unlike its counterpart of 1914, this was an army unprepared for a major war; the government had not even authorised its formation until February 1939, since they had wanted to keep Britain out of any major European conflict. Because of this, most of the expansion of the services in the late 1930s had been designed to improve the security of the United Kingdom itself, or the Empire, rather than to support an ally in mainland Europe.

This hastily organised field army was intended to operate on the northern flank of the French army as in 1914, but it took several months before it reached its full strength. This time, fortunately, there was no massive German attack in the early weeks of the war, and as time passed without any sign of action on the Western Front the media of the day coined the phrase 'the Phoney War'. This breathing space gave the opportunity to build defences, dubbed the Gort Line after the BEF's commander, Lord Gort of Limerick, VC, and to train for the coming war.

There were three Ulster infantry battalions in the BEF – 2nd Royal Inniskilling Fusiliers, 2nd Royal Ulster Rifles and 1st Royal Irish Fusiliers, as well as an anti-aircraft artillery brigade – 3rd (Ulster) AA Brigade – from which one regiment had gone to the Middle East.

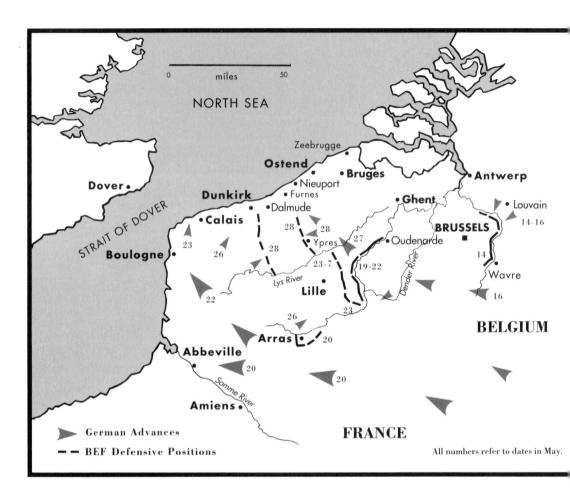

NORTH SEA

0   miles   50

Dover •

STRAIT OF DOVER

Zeebrugge

Ostend •

• Bruges

• Antwerp

• Nieuport

• Furnes

• Ghent

• Louvain

14-16

Dunkirk •

• Dalmude

BRUSSELS ■

• Calais

28

28

Ypres

27

• Oudenarde

14

Boulogne •

23

26

28

23-7

19-22

Wavre

22

Lys River

• Lille

Dender River

16

BELGIUM

26

23

Arras •

20

20

Abbeville •

Somme River

20

Amiens •

FRANCE

German Advances

BEF Defensive Positions

All numbers refer to dates in May.

In April 1940 the Germans invaded Norway and Denmark, quickly overrunning both countries. Then on 10 May, a bright spring morning, the so-called Phoney War came to an end with a German attack that was so sudden and so devastating that it was to lead to the evacuation of the BEF through a number of French ports, the best known, of course, being Dunkirk:

As they said in those days, the balloon went up in Belgium. On 10 May the Germans attacked Holland and Belgium. We were turned about . . . we had no transport so we marched from the Somme to Lille. The transport had gone ahead of us into Belgium and we stayed at night at farms and places like that. The weather was beautiful so it was quite pleasant. We got transport from around Lille and went up south of Brussels and met the Germans at a place called Hals, and eventually after a bit of skirmishing and shooting we had to withdraw because by that time it was evident that things weren't quite right.

Lieutenant Billy Megaw, 2nd Royal Inniskilling Fusiliers

The first Ulster unit to meet the Germans had been 2nd Royal Ulster Rifles, which had been part of a British force ordered into Belgium in an attempt to stop the German advance. Several leading units of the force had found their way into Belgium blocked by Belgian customs officers demanding their papers; entry was achieved by ramming the customs barriers and driving on. Then, on 14 May, the Rifles came into contact with the German army and for five weary days they fought against heavy odds:

We were rushed off straight up to Louvain in Belgium. Our battalion headquarters was in the cathedral and our front line was in the railway station. The Germans were on one platform and the Rifles were on the other platform – as close as that.

Colour-Sergeant Dick Connell, 2nd Royal Ulster Rifles

The Rifles held their positions at Louvain under continued German attacks for five days, during which Dick Connell saw a number of his friends killed, until the collapse of the French army forced the British Expeditionary Force to begin its retreat. That advance into Belgium by the BEF could very nearly

Carriers of 1st Royal Irish Fusiliers moving through Gavrelle, near Le Mans, in October 1939.

have proved fatal; the German attack on 10 May had been part of a strategy to quickly destroy the French army in the Maginot Line between France and Germany, as well as eliminate the British Expeditionary Force by striking towards the channel ports, thus cutting off their supply routes and line of retreat. The BEF would have been surrounded, with no option but to surrender, while the bulk of the French army would have been outflanked and hopelessly outmanoeuvred.

The Germans had taken a British idea – a fast-moving attack by tanks and mobile infantry, supported by fighter-bombers which would crash through the enemy lines and sweep round to attack from the rear – and adapted it to German strategy, a strategy that had failed because of a British Expeditionary Force in 1914. This new plan was dubbed *blitzkrieg* – lightning war – by the British media.

The German task was made even simpler. At this early stage of the war, they had not only more infantry, but more tanks, better tanks, and could make better use of them. In addition, the execution of this outflanking movement, or sickle sweep, was the type of manoeuvre at which the Wehrmacht excelled:

> Ours wasn't such a big force altogether against the might of the German army. I saw the German army going down one road and them waving to us on another road – they were that sure they had us. They had a terrific army coming right in. There were hundreds of tanks . . . there were motorcycles and sidecars with a machine-gun mounted on the sidecar. That was how they came in for a quick run . . . and they had all the armour and everything that you could name.
>
> **Fusilier David Laird**, *1st Royal Irish Fusiliers*

On the occasion described by David Laird, the commanding officer of the Royal Irish Fusiliers, Lieutenant-Colonel Guy Gough, MC, was fortunate to escape death when his staff car was riddled by machine-gun fire from passing German motorcyclists. Gough's orderly was hit, but he himself was out of the car studying his maps and was uninjured.

One of the aims of the German command was to create confusion, thereby reducing their opponents' morale. The Germans' speed and overwhelming superiority in equipment certainly helped to thicken the 'fog of war' in France and to destroy French army morale:

We thought that we were every bit as good as they were but we didn't realise how many tanks and how many aeroplanes they would produce and how few we had. We never saw our own tanks.

We came through up to the Scarpe, through the village, and there were enormous French tanks. It was night-time, beautiful weather, and the Frenchmen were sitting smoking round behind us, and we marched through the village and someone said, 'We're OK, we've got those boys behind us.' We never saw them again.

There was total confusion. There was one crossroads . . . where a battalion – no, four battalions were going four different directions! It wasn't very heartening. You just marched on, that was all there was to it, and when you were told to stop and dig . . . by that time we didn't even have shovels.

Lieutenant Billy Megaw

Shovels had been thrown away by frustrated infantrymen, anxious to lighten their burden on the interminable marches. As for armoured support, the BEF, although it had ten divisions of infantry, had only one brigade of tanks when the Germans struck; it was hardly surprising that Lieutenant Megaw never saw his own armour.

German tactics proved completely successful and caused the almost total collapse of the French army. France had devoted a huge proportion of its military budget in the 1930s to constructing the Maginot Line on the Franco-German border and confidently believed the line would keep the Germans out. However, the German army simply went around the Maginot Line, through Belgium, to invade France; the Franco-Belgian border had not been fortified for diplomatic reasons. The BEF was forced to look after itself and began retreating to the Channel coast. This was made doubly difficult by the fact that British soldiers were not the only people on the move into France:

The Belgian civilians, the whole of the Belgian population [it seemed] was on the move. Now, they had been occupied in the First War by the Germans and hated them and had no wish to be occupied again. So they put their bundles under their arms and they said they were getting out because the Germans had already gone in by that time, although we didn't know it, to Brussels.

And there was a strange procession of the well-off first, in their big cars, and then the not-so-well-off in carts, and then the poor people on their feet carrying their possessions. It was a very pathetic business. The Germans by that time had complete superiority in the air and they were bombing and machine-gunning everybody, including us.

Lieutenant Billy Megaw

The road along which the Rifles were marching 'was absolutely jammed tight with vehicles and handcarts and dogcarts and all sorts of animals. And every inch of the ground and the footpath along the road was impossible to get through' (Dick Connell).

Some sights along those roads were so pathetic and so heart-rending that they remain unforgettable and are indelibly imprinted in many soldiers' minds:

. . . we marched past one little baby sitting in the middle of the road and the mother dead beside it and, really, I can see her yet. And there was nothing we could do but march on. It was happening all round us.

Lieutenant Billy Megaw

The retreat began on 19 May for the Royal Ulster Rifles; it was to be another twelve days before they reached Dunkirk. There was little opportunity to sleep or eat along the way. In fact, eating often became a matter of improvisation because supply lines had broken down in the confusion:

C Company came to a farm and that was where they had their company headquarters. There was no food about, but there was a big fat pig and one of my riflemen – a fella called Waddell from Limavady who was a butcher – we got this big pig and Waddell sorted the pig out and made it into a kind of an Irish stew. And there was enough to feed – well, we had about 140 [men]. Everybody got a good meal out of that.

Colour-Sergeant Dick Connell

During the retreat several attempts were made to block the German onslaught. The Royal Irish Fusiliers held the Bethune-La Bassée Canal for three days from 23 May against the German 7th Panzer Division, commanded by Major General Erwin Rommel, later to become famous in North Africa as the 'Desert Fox'. The Faughs found that their German opponents were unwilling to fight at night and were also very poor in small group tactics. Only the weight of German numbers and their superiority in tanks carried the position for Rommel's men; by that stage the Irish Fusiliers had been relieved.

At the same time 2nd Royal Inniskilling Fusiliers had fallen back to the Escaut Canal and then on to the Ypres-Comines Canal at Holebeek, where their task was to hold up the German advance and allow the BEF to retreat to Dunkirk. On the banks of the Ypres-Comines Canal Billy Megaw was wounded. The Skins had taken up positions on the railway line and could see the Germans coming. Suddenly, in the midst of the tension as bombs and shells fell around them, Megaw recalled:

> . . . along came a train from Ypres full of civilians – women and children . . . . They went on – how far they got I don't know – but we were badly shelled and eventually the Germans attacked round us.
>
> The Cameronians were on the right. We were on the railway embankment and it was very difficult. You had to put your head and shoulders up over the rails to fire, and the Germans were infiltrating and evidently some of them had got through a culvert underneath the railway embankment and they ran away back of us, and I think that's where I got hit – from these people who were behind us by that time.
>
> We had only just one single line of one company, three platoons up, and company headquarters was further back in a little village.

The wounded Megaw was brought back to an advanced dressing station of the Royal Army Medical Corps (RAMC) – a commandeered house – 'and from there, by luck, I got to Dunkirk'. The luck element, reckoned Megaw, came about after a friend of his, Geoff Cocksedge, the carrier platoon commander who had also been wounded, was apparently the last to be evacuated from the dressing station by ambulance. The ambulances had been coming along from time to time amid very heavy shelling, and when Cocksedge was taken away Megaw heard a sergeant say to the doctor, 'That's the last one, sir.' He resigned himself to his fate, which he reckoned

Top: Dunkirk in flames. This photograph is one of a series taken by Lieutenant (later Major General) Bala Bredin of the Royal Ulster Rifles as his battalion was being evacuated from Dunkirk.

Left: 'Stukas are always petrifyingly terrifying.' A Luftwaffe photograph of a Ju87B Stuka as it drops its bomb-load at the bottom of its dive.

would be capture, for 'by that time to say things were a bit vague was to put it mildly'.

Fortunately for Billy Megaw, another ambulance did arrive minutes later. He was stretchered into it to begin a three-day trek across France. In one way he was lucky; he had transport when the vast majority of soldiers had to make their way to the coast on foot. But everyone, civilian and soldier alike, was under the ever-present threat of attack from the German air force – the Luftwaffe – which had complete mastery of the air over France. This air superiority allowed the Luftwaffe's Ju87 dive-bombers – known as Stukas – to operate at ease, bombing and machine-gunning troops and civilians. These aircraft carried out their bombing attacks in steep dives, accompanied by a horrific wailing sound: 'Stukas are always petrifyingly frightening. They had things on their wings which made them scream. But they were [particularly] terrifying . . . to the civilians on the roads who went absolutely astray . . . especially the children. That was the most dreadful business' (Billy Megaw).

While the Inniskillings and the Irish Fusiliers were making their way to Dunkirk, the Ulster Rifles found themselves at La Panne, a small town on the north coast of France from where they were hoping to make it back home. Arriving in La Panne in the middle of the night, a scene of confusion and chaos greeted the Rifles: 'Everybody was shouting and Redcaps [military policemen] saying, "Go there" and "Go there" and go everywhere. There was nobody really in charge' (Dick Connell).

Connell got down a defile to the beach with a number of his companions, where a pier had been improvised by driving lorries into the sea and putting planks along the tops of the lorries. Telling his fellow riflemen to 'Keep with me', Colour-Sergeant Connell made his way to the pier. There the intention was to walk out to where the small boats, which were intended to take them to the warships, could pick them up: 'But we stood on that gangway for hours until it was nearly the middle of the next day and couldn't get anything at all. And the tide came in. Of course, we were up to our waists in water' (Dick Connell).

At that stage the Rifles' commanding officer, Lieutenant-Colonel 'Gandhi' Knox, decided to get his men off the pier and out of La Panne, with the call, 'All riflemen this way.' Addressing them, Colonel Knox explained that because they were unlikely to get off the beach, he had decided they would march to Dunkirk, about nine or ten miles away. After a mile they moved onto a firm road, on which better progress was possible. On the road another of the transport men, Frank Byrne, a Dubliner, said to Dick Connell, 'Come on, we'll get one of these vehicles and see if we can get through.' And so the pair commandeered an abandoned army staff car.

Byrne, the transport sergeant and a mechanic, examined the car and reckoned that he could make it roadworthy. He worked on it for a time, then he and Connell got in and drove on; however, the steering was not responding properly, and every half-hour the men had to stop to hammer the road-wheels round in order to make the car travel in a straight line. The pair travelled for 'a good mile or two in that', after which the road became too difficult to drive on. They abandoned the car and joined the marching riflemen, who were close behind them on the road, so slow had been the car's progress.

Soon after, the road became so blocked up that the battalion had to move back onto the beach:

> It was the early evening and . . . three or four Messerschmitts came zooming along the beach and just rattling away at everybody, and Frank Byrne and I dived into a shell-hole, or just a hole in the ground, and a minute or two later I said, 'They're away now – come on, we'll go', and there was no answer. So I gave Frank a dig and said 'Come on', and he rolled over . . . and he was dead.
>
> *Colour-Sergeant Dick Connell*

Frank Byrne was one of the many casualties on the way to Dunkirk. By this stage in the campaign the High Command had decided to withdraw the British Expeditionary Force from France in order to save it from annihilation. The plan was to regroup and continue the war. (The idea was, in fact, to land once again in France, but further west, in order to bolster the French government.)

The immediate result of this decision was that over 250,000 men were forced into Dunkirk for the evacuation. For the man on the ground the lasting impression was one of total chaos and danger:

> Then the dawn broke, and we saw the catastrophe . . . ambulances, trucks just being hit on the beach – men lying [dead]. Nobody gave a damn whether you were a brigadier or a general. And then we saw the ships out there and they'd organised a pier of vehicles and planks so that we'd get out to the navy ships. The navy ships were getting

bombed that much the Germans were just coming over and sticking the bombs down the funnels.

Bandsman John Donovan, Royal Ulster Rifles

While the Luftwaffe attacked the hastily organised evacuation fleet, the soldiers on dry land were ordered to destroy their vehicles, artillery and heavy equipment, in order to prevent them from falling into enemy hands. Lorries were driven into fields outside Dunkirk, their engine-blocks smashed and the vehicles set on fire, leaving the soldiers to march down to the shore. Not all the destruction, however, was carried out efficiently, for the German army was able to salvage much British equipment, some of which was still in use in France when the Allies returned in 1944. In the midst of all this destruction, a company of Royal Irish Fusiliers found, to their surprise, that a bus service had been organised from the outskirts of Dunkirk to take them to the evacuation beaches. During all this frenetic activity, priority was given to getting the wounded on board ship, but many of them had to make it on foot:

> The military police were stopping trucks getting into Dunkirk and the military policemen hauled me out and said, 'Anybody who can walk, there's the place to go.' So, I'd been hit in the legs but I managed to, as they say in Ulster, be oxter-cogged along until I got to the pier which was still standing by that time, although there were great big holes in it. And don't ask me how I got up it, but I got up it, and one of our British destroyers was there, and again I was helped on by a great big seaman and put in a lovely bed and I never knew another thing until we got to Dover. That was the end of that and we'll never, of course, forget the Royal Navy – the way they came right in. They lost [a lot of ships]. The destroyer I got out on, they say, bought it the next trip.
>
> *Lieutenant Billy Megaw*

The fireworks were . . . everywhere – bombs and bullets, aircraft bullets, flying in all directions. And old Gandhi Knox was really good. He said, 'Follow me, boys', and we headed down towards the harbour, and in the harbour there was a pleasure-boat pulled alongside, so we all dived onto it. And Gandhi said, 'Everybody who's got a Bren gun get up on top', because the Stukas were coming down and the Stuka was diving straight at the boat but not hitting anything. It hit the sea several times and the ship bounced up and down. And it hit the land and everybody on the top deck [was] blazing away with their Bren guns.

Colour-Sergeant Dick Connell

By the time John Donovan and his companions got onto the beach, there appeared to be no small boats left. However, gunners from an artillery battery searched the dunes, found a boat and brought it down to the beach. Donovan and his comrades – Gussie Ward from Belfast and Jack Ennis from Dublin – climbed into the boat, which had been set afloat but was so crowded that men were clinging to the sides. A senior officer ordered the boat to get off and they began their journey towards the big ships.

Donovan was unimpressed by the way in which some aspects of the evacuation were handled, especially the 'shuttle service' of small rowing boats from the beach:

They got on board [the ships] and left them [the rowing boats] there. So we come along, and there's no boats for us. The drill should have been ten on the boat, five [to] go out and five [to] come back – like in a shuttle service. But that never happened.

So anyway, we got this boat and started pulling out and heading for the open sea. All of a sudden this voice of authority, a second lieutenant from some English crowd, raised his voice and said, 'We have to get organised as we may be at sea for a week or two weeks.' . . . Got romantic he did . . . we might finish up in America.

Bandsman John Donovan

The young officer even offered to take all his companions to the best hotel in London for a meal when they got home. No one was surprised at not getting their meal; they never saw the officer again after they reached England.

Now, however, the exhausted soldiers, who had hardly slept for three weeks, were trying to row. 'They were fagged out,' said Donovan, 'the boat was going round in circles.' They were not yet free of France; as they rowed wearily away, the men were challenged by a Royal Navy patrol boat, which drew alongside and took them on board, where they collapsed in exhaustion. Before falling asleep, Donovan asked where the boat was going. Expecting to hear 'Dover' or 'Folkestone', or some other English south-coast town, he was amazed when the answer was 'Dunkirk'. He woke up when the boat was hit by shrapnel to find himself back in Dunkirk, which appeared to be like 'a scene out of Dante's Inferno. People were screaming and the place was in flames.' It was a relief when the boat finally left for England.

> I don't know how long . . . we were getting back. It was hours and hours . . . . I remember when we got onto the [harbour] . . . at Folkestone . . . an old lady coming forward with three wee china cups on her fingers and a jug of tea and a big plate of scones and things. And she came over to me and she said, 'Would you like a cup of tea?' I hadn't seen anything to eat for about a week or so, so I just took the jug in one hand and the plate in the other and went and sat down. And there was this old lady standing with the three cups dangling on her fingers.
>
> *Fusilier David Laird*

On arrival in England each soldier was given a card on which to write home that he had been evacuated safely. Men were then moved to reception depots, fed and given leave, after which they were ordered to return to their own units, for many had become separated in the confusion. A few found themselves back in France, with the small force commanded by an Ulsterman, General Brooke, which, it was hoped, might resuscitate French morale. That hope was not to be realised, and even the offer of a Franco-British Union could not stop the French from seeking an armistice. French resistance ended on 25 June, by which time the final British evacuation, from Cherbourg and St Malo, had been completed.

The evacuation of the Allied forces from Dunkirk has been hailed by many over the years as a moral victory. That was so even at the time, for Winston Churchill, who had replaced Chamberlain as prime minister on that fateful day of 10 May, called the evacuation 'a miracle of deliverance', while the *Daily Mirror* used the headline 'BLOODY MARVELLOUS' – the first occasion on which a British paper had printed a swear word. After all, almost 200,000 British, and just under 140,000 French troops, had been rescued, although over 2,000 guns, 60,000 vehicles and more than 75,000 tons of ammunition had been left behind, together with more than 400,000 tons of general stores.

After Dunkirk some soldiers looked on the evacuation as a kind of triumph, much to the chagrin of General Montgomery. Monty was annoyed to see 'soldiers walking around London with a coloured, embroidered flash on their sleeve with the title "Dunkirk"', in obvious imitation of a German battle-honours system. It was soon stopped. In one sense, however, it was true that there had been something to celebrate; after all, the entire BEF could easily have been cut off in France and Belgium and destroyed. For many of the ordinary soldiers, however, the lasting impression differed from that of triumph and success.

And so we reached those beaches, and Gaul in ruins stood,
La Panne in flames behind us, Dunkirk ten miles ahead,
We fought a rearguard action, a war of untold fame,
But somewhere along the line, someone was to blame.

Bandsman John Donovan

Oh, it most obviously was a defeat. We were sent packing. But the discipline and the spirit of the army – they got us out, plus the Royal Navy and the wee boats that came in. But there's no talking around it – it was a tremendous defeat.

Lieutenant Billy Megaw

I'd been a professional soldier and I'd been trained to fight wars, and the British Army fought wars, and here we were, running away . . . . I couldn't understand that, but to me the worst part was going back into Dunkirk when this naval patrol picked us up. It was like Dante's Inferno; it'll live in my memory forever, and I heard the squeals. Squeals – you hear pigs squealing, you know. It was a crescendo of sound – of, of men in agony. I wouldn't like to go to hell, and that's what it was.

Bandsman John Donovan

For Valour

Instituted in 1856, the Victoria Cross is the highest British bravery award. Any rank of any service can earn it 'for valour', and it is recognised throughout the world as perhaps the greatest gallantry award anywhere. In the history of the Victoria Cross, however, the story of how **Captain Harold Ervine-Andrews** won his medal has few equals.

Ervine-Andrews was born in Keadue, County Cavan, on 29 July 1911. Educated at Stoneyhurst College, Lancashire, and Sandhurst he was commissioned into the East Lancashire Regiment. On 31 May 1940 he commanded a company of 2nd East Lancashires near Dunkirk. His battalion was part of the rearguard around Dunkirk – the men who made it possible for most of the BEF to get away. That night he had forty men, all that were left from his company, to cover the battalion's retreat. The building which Ervine-Andrews's company had been defending was set alight, but instead of ordering a withdrawal the Irishman told his soldiers that they were going to charge the Germans – less than forty against 500!

As the Germans crossed the Canal de Bergues at dawn on 1 June, Ervine-Andrews led his men in what should have been a suicidal attack; the enemy, however, were so taken by surprise that they fell back. Ervine-Andrews then dashed to a barn with his soldiers, climbed onto the roof and opened fire on the Germans. He shot seventeen with rifle fire and many more with Bren-gun fire; when ammunition ran low he and his men attacked the Germans with fists, feet and even teeth, as one survivor told the *Daily Telegraph*.

Faced with this ferocity, the Germans drew back completely. In the short calm that followed, Captain Ervine-Andrews was able to send his wounded back in the sole surviving carrier. Only eight men remained with him by this time, but he was still not finished. Determined to lead his men to safety he:

. . . collected the remaining eight men of his company from this forward position and when almost surrounded, led them back to the cover afforded by the company to the rear, swimming or wading up to the chin in water for over a mile.

Taken from the citation for his VC, *London Gazette*, 30 July 1940.

Ervine-Andrews and his men reached safety and were evacuated from the Dunkirk beaches, the East Lancashires being one of the last infantry units to leave. Harold Marcus Ervine-Andrews had become the first British soldier to win the Victoria Cross in the Second World War.

The British Army's first VC of the war. Captain Harold Marcus Ervine-Andrews, VC, of the East Lancashire Regiment, a native of Co. Cavan, won his medal in a rearguard action outside Dunkirk.

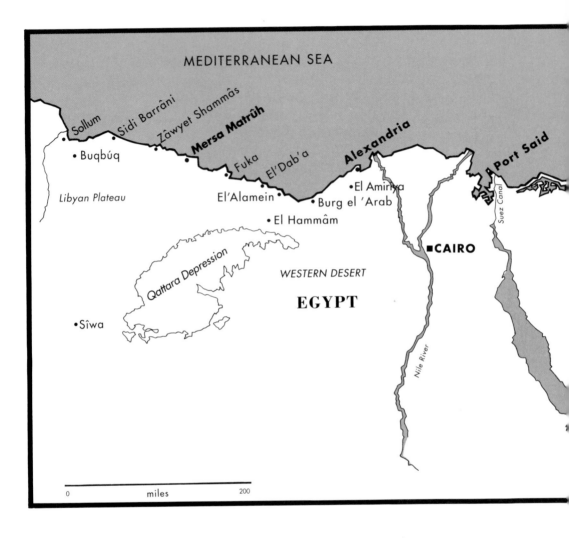

MEDITERRANEAN SEA

Sollum

Sidi Barrâni

Zâwyet Shammâs

Mersa Matrûh

• Buqbúq

Fuka

El'Dab'a

Alexandria

Port Said

Libyan Plateau

El'Alamein •

• El Amiriya

• Burg el 'Arab

• El Hammâm

Suez Canal

Qattara Depression

WESTERN DESERT

CAIRO

EGYPT

•Sîwa

Nile River

| 0 | miles | 200 |

3

The Desert War

We had sixty-five nights when we were raided every night.

SUNDAY, 13th of April 1941: travelled through the night; very cold; no sleep. Arrive in Alexandria at 6.30 am. We go to Mustapha Barracks for grub; two eggs, bread and tea. We are fallen out for a few hours. I get a wash, shave and a haircut. My clothes are filthy and I feel the same. Two-Four Battery boys meet up with our lads. What a celebration! – plenty of drink. Our lads commandeer a native band and parade the station platform – pipes, drums, etc. I think the natives believe we have escaped from a loony-bin. We finally pull out of Sidi Gabr station at 12.30 pm.

Monday, 14th of April 1941: we know we are now heading for the Western Desert . . .

These words are from the diary of **Gunner John Ormsby**, 25 Heavy Anti-Aircraft Battery. On Easter Sunday, 1941, his battery had been ordered to the Western Desert for the second time in less than a year.

John Ormsby was one of many Ulstermen who took part in the Desert War, which began on 10 June 1940 and lasted for almost three years. His battery was part of 9th (Londonderry) Heavy Anti-Aircraft Regiment, Royal Artillery, raised in early 1939 before the outbreak of war and comprised of civilian volunteers and several former regular soldiers. Many came from families who had known the loss of a father or an uncle during the First World War. John Ormsby had been named after an uncle killed in the Irish Guards at the first Battle of Ypres on 1 November 1914.

War came to North Africa when the Italian dictator, Benito Mussolini, decided that the British were completely beaten after the fall of France.

51

Il Duce believed that he could march into Egypt from the Italian colony of Libya and add Egypt to Italy's empire. His generals tried to persuade him not to attack; they believed their army was so poorly equipped that even the small British forces in Egypt could hold them off. Mussolini had his own way, however, declaring war on 10 June.

Soon Italian bombers were attacking the port of Alexandria, which was defended by 9th (Londonderry) Heavy Anti-Aircraft Regiment. In September the Italian 10th Army, under Marshal Rudolfo Graziani, moved into Egypt. Graziani stopped his advance after capturing the small town of Sidi Barrani on the coast and began to prepare defensive positions.

In December 1940 General Wavell, who commanded the British Middle East Forces, launched a counter-attack called Operation COMPASS. In a matter of weeks his Western Desert Force, under an Irishman, General Richard O'Connor, had destroyed the much larger Italian army and taken over 100,000 prisoners, among whom were a number of Italian generals including Graziani. The Italians were rapidly forced back towards Tripoli and the campaign in North Africa looked to be over.

Then two things happened which significantly affected the course of the Desert War. Firstly, Prime Minister Winston Churchill decided to send British troops to Greece to counter an Italian invasion. The soldiers sent to Greece were from O'Connor's small army, which was forced to halt its advance at El Agheila. Wavell had opposed the move of troops to Greece, but was powerless to prevent them going. At this stage Hitler decided to aid his Italian ally, and a German army corps – the Deutsches Afrika Korps – was sent to Libya under Major General Erwin Rommel, who was to become known as the Desert Fox.

Shortly after arriving in Africa – and against orders – Rommel attacked the British at El Agheila and began to push the weakened British corps back towards Egypt. On Good Friday, 1941 the Afrika Korps crashed through the Halfaya Pass into Egypt, and every available unit was sent up to the desert to try to stop its advance. On Easter Sunday morning, 25 Heavy Anti-Aircraft Battery arrived back in Alexandria after nearly a year in Sudan; the battery was ordered to Mersa Matruh and was given two hours' notice: 'It was no surprise, really, when we got on board that rickety old train for Mersa, but I didn't anticipate what we were going to get when we arrived there – just how bad the conditions were' (*Gunner John Ormsby*).

Sergeant Eric Wilson remembered their first night in bombed buildings and how he longed for the dawn in order to warm up. After almost a year in the tropical heat of Sudan, the cold of a desert night seemed unbearable, and 'even the flies were welcome in that situation'.

Flies were not their only companions at Mersa:

My particular memory of Mersa Matruh is [of] a flea-infested place. It was absolutely hopeless. We did our blankets with paraffin oil to try to kill them, and one poor fellow, Billy Peoples, mixed paraffin and creosote and rubbed his body with it with the end result that he nearly went mad. It took the skin off him and he also happened to be a very hairy individual. Anyway, your first job in the morning was to strip off all your clothes and crack the boys. I remember distinctly counting eighteen on my clothes when I took them off. You had to sleep with all your clothes on you because we had still only one blanket each.

Gunner John Ormsby

Mersa Matruh was regarded as the last line of defence for the Nile Delta and Suez Canal. It was vital that it be held, and soldiers from Britain, India and Australia were sent to its defence. Many were ill-prepared for the climate, especially those who had arrived from the tropical heat of Sudan. Although day-time in the desert was searingly hot, the nights were unbelievably cold:

Most of us had togged ourselves out with pieces of canvas or whatever we could get our hands on to keep ourselves up off the sand. With your blanket and an Italian groundsheet and your W.D. groundsheet you could usually keep reasonably warm, but when it came on to November and December, and through what we would call the winter months in this country, you very often lay down at night with all your clothes on and your greatcoat and you'd wake up in the morning feeling quite cold, especially if you couldn't have anything over your head, which we seldom had. That was because the dew came down at night and saturated everything, left everything absolutely soaking, and this seemed to make you feel even colder.

When you were throwing these bits and pieces on the back of the three-tonner or the Matador, sometimes people like Sergeant McClure would be around and you'd be wondering if he was going to tell us to take that off the lorry. We persevered and one way and another we

Afrika Korps on the move. Rommel's forces advance into Egypt and across the Western Desert.

Prepare for action! A gun crew of 25 Battery are ready for the order to fire. Ammunition-bearers already hold further rounds for the crew, and the gun commander can be seen with his arm raised in the background; when he brings down his arm the gun will be fired.

learned, as the months and the years passed, that we had to look after number one.

Gunner Bertie Cuthbert

Although the desert and its discomforts would never become home to them, the men of 25 Battery would learn to live with it and would adapt to its hostile environment. One man who seemed unaffected by climate and conditions was **Gunner J. J. Doherty**, one of the battery's dispatch riders. **Jim Canning** recalled how J. J.'s boots always looked ready for a parade ground, while most others had allowed their footwear to deteriorate. Gunner Doherty had been a regular soldier in the Royal Irish Fusiliers, with previous service in Egypt and Sudan so that the heat was not unbearable to him, while his smart turnout was a reflection of the high standards of the Royal Irish Fusiliers.

Food was another of the desert's discomforts, and no soldier would forget its accompanying monotony:

> The food you got in the desert consisted of bully-beef and hard biscuits. Some of the biscuits that we ate in the desert, especially in the early days, had been canned in 1916 and were stored in underground buildings . . . . When one of these tins was opened you could smell the malt from the biscuits at least a quarter of a mile away. That's not an exaggeration, and apparently it was the amount of malt in these biscuits that gave us the energy to survive.
>
> The bully-beef didn't come out of the tin in the desert in one block as it would do in this country. It came out like a stew, and you could have supped it with a spoon rather than cut it with a knife. And when you were trying to eat this bully-beef and biscuits the flies seemed to get the signal to get to action stations, and you had to be damned careful that you didn't swallow a few flies along with the bite of bully-beef.
>
> *Gunner Bertie Cuthbert*

Two-Five Battery was in action from the word go and had its first casualty a week after arriving at Matruh. The incident occurred just after tea one evening:

> I am resting in my tent at 6.30 pm when heavy explosions out to sea bring me running to my post. I spot a plane flying high coming towards us. We get on target, a Ju88. He lets go six bombs that pass over us

and fall on mainland. We fire ten rounds. I reckon they are too low. F
Section fire four rounds. The bombs straddled our radar site, wounding
five of our lads and killing Driver Thomas Porter who was just driving
into the site.

Gunner John Ormsby

I was watching the plane . . . with spyglasses, dropping the bombs,
and then I discovered afterwards that Tommy Porter, the driver, had
been killed.

Gunner George Lapsley

The bomber had dropped a stick of bombs in a straight line, straddling the
radar site controlling the battery's guns:

The only thing that was worrying Tommy when he was severely
wounded was who would drive his lorry now. When Sir Basil
McFarland [the battery's second-in-command] went to see him he
asked Sir Basil, 'Who'll drive my lorry now, sir?' That and 'Don't
tell me mother' [were] his last words.

Gunner George Lapsley

As the campaign in the desert moved back and forth, part of 25 Battery
moved to the Libyan border while the remainder stayed at Mersa Matruh.
During the summer of 1941 enemy bombers paid special attention to Matruh
Harbour, where the gunners found sleep a rarity:

Most of the raids were at night-time. You could almost time the first
raid; it came in, I think, about 8.45 or 9.00 in the evening and that
went on, just wave after wave – not many planes in each wave, about
five or six planes – and they kept that going until about 3.00 or 4.00
in the morning, so that you were on the guns all that time.

You got the odd break, and I remember Davy Sinclair [one of the
battery's cooks] would always try and get tea for us, but he had a petrol
cooker and the noise it made – well, the boys didn't like it because
they couldn't hear the planes coming in then, so he had to stop. That
was very rough and then, of course, you got maybe an hour or two
[of] sleep, but you were up the next morning, for the guns had to be
cleaned and made ready for action again.

You got alarms during the day, mostly for reconnaissance planes coming in very high, but it kept you on your toes all the time. I remember the night that we fired an awful lot of rounds. Why that happened I'm not sure now, but they must have kept their planes coming in for a longer period.

It was very vital that Matruh Harbour was kept open for the sake of Tobruk, and I think we can safely say that we did a very good job there under very trying circumstances.

Sergeant Ernie McClure

The port of Tobruk in Libya had been held by the Australians against the Germans and Italians and was under siege, which would last until late November. Tobruk could only be supplied by sea, and many of the supplies passed through the small harbour at Matruh. Understandably, the Germans wanted to knock out Matruh, and it was the job of the anti-aircraft gunners and searchlight crews to prevent them doing so. Some German pilots were prepared to go to almost any lengths to overcome the defences in their attempts to destroy the harbour, including direct attacks on the defences themselves:

The master searchlight was just behind us on the site about thirty yards from the guns, and the boys on it were very, very good at their job. So, everything that came in they picked it up and when they picked it up the other searchlights held it, and he [the master light] searched for something else.

But one night a boy came in and the beam caught him and the German just heeled over and dived down the beam. They were trying to put the master light out, you see, but the boys held onto him. You just held your breath until he pulled out and we loaded one-point-five shrapnel, and as soon as he pulled out we all fired, and I think the boy didn't go up again.

Gunner Miles Stott

The other half of 25 Battery were at Sidi Barrani, near the Libyan border, defending Desert Air Force landing-strips. This made the battery a target for German and Italian fighter pilots, who would often machine-gun the strips. During one such attack John Ormsby had a particularly close shave:

I always saved a small drop of tea in my mug in order to shave. I had a hole dug in the ground fifty yards from the gun – myself and Jim McMorris shared this hole. I was lathering my face as best I could with the tea and we heard the hum of these planes again and I shouted down to the command post, 'What are those?' 'Aw, they're our own, you're all right.' Next thing, down they started, the cannons opening fire.

Well, I headed like the hammers of hell for the command post. But there was a gun in my path, and I caught the muzzle of the gun and dropped into the pit, and at that moment she fired. Apparently Sergeant Loughlin had given the order to fire. Sammy McKinney was the firing man on the gun and he'd seen me running straight for the muzzle of the gun so he held his arm. The sergeant said, 'Damn ye, fire!' . . . Sammy still held on, I dropped in and the minute I dropped into the pit she went off, with the result that I got my eardrums burst.

But when we went back later I found, whether it had been incendiary bullets or not, because I didn't smoke, my kit was on fire. My paybook I just salvaged from my shirt. I had an old topi sitting on top of the kit on the outside of this hole and I still have the paybook to this day with the burnt edges. One chappie was hit in that raid, he was an Englishman called Jones. He threw himself under a lorry that was some distance from the guns, and as far as I know he got six bullets up the side of his body. It was the worst place in the world to go, under a vehicle.

The fighters on the drome were caught by surprise. Some of them got off, and I recall one of our chappies who was manning a Bren gun let fly at this plane coming across low, and it happened to be one of our own. Bits of the tail flew off her – it was a Hurricane belonging to ourselves, unfortunately; but he didn't do [the pilot] any harm as far as I know, for he got away. But it was an experience never to be forgotten.

Things were no easier in Matruh, which was under constant bombardment:

I remember Mersa Matruh as probably the toughest period of the war from my point of view . . . . I think we had sixty-five nights when we were raided every night. Eventually, the health broke down, for we got no sleep and we were under severe pressure, and so many had health problems that they had to pull us out . . . . So, for me, that was the roughest part of the war.

Sergeant Ernie McClure

Arrival of the water wagon. Water was scarce in the desert and strictly rationed. These soldiers greet the arrival of a water truck with obvious enthusiasm.

Bad health was an abiding problem, caused by the heat, poor living conditions and an almost complete lack of fresh fruit and vegetables. There was also a shortage of water. The normal water ration was one gallon per man per day, but each soldier did not receive a full gallon for himself. The cooks received half the ration for cooking, leaving the soldier with a half-gallon, but even that was an optimistic assessment – there would inevitably be spillages and evaporation. If the battery received its full ration on a particular day, the most water a soldier was issued would have been a half-gallon. With these four pints of water, he had to wash, shave, brew tea and keep his clothes clean! Shaving was always compulsory, mainly because a bearded face did not allow an anti-gas respirator to do its job properly. Small wonder, then, that men adopted the trick described by John Ormsby of saving some tea in the bottom of a mug for shaving, or that unusual methods of laundering were tried, including the use of petrol as a form of dry-cleaning. Finally, the water that the men did receive had been treated with salt and chlorine, leaving it with an unpleasant taste and unappealing appearance.

When a deep well was discovered at Sidi Barrani, the men of 25 Battery thought that their water problems might be alleviated. After a short time, however, the well dried up. Efforts to restore the supply included lowering a man into the well to find the cause of the problem. When he came up to report the presence of several dead dogs, the use of the well was rapidly abandoned!

The absence of fresh fruit and vegetables from the diet undoubtedly caused the most uncomfortable health problem – desert sores. At one stage, this unpleasant affliction caused a quarter of the battery to be hospitalised:

> You could actually give your skin a rub on any part of your body and the skin lifted and . . . white bubbles of water came out and from [then] on it started. There was no healing of it at all.
>
> One chap, Bob Dunwoody, had a very, very severe one on his ankle, and it ended up that you could see the actual joint, and the medical people wanted to take the leg off. Bob wouldn't agree to taking the leg off. He was taken to hospital, right enough, and I met him in later years in Portrush and I said, 'Bob, I see you still have your leg.' And . . . he [said], 'Thank goodness I stood firm.'
>
> And they were talking at that time [in North Africa] of transferring him back to Britain, or [to] a cooler climate where he would get

the type of rations that would help him. It was certain vitamins that we were lacking, especially from the green vegetables, which we didn't get.

Gunner John Ormsby

Some men were fortunate enough to go through the period in the desert without suffering sores. George Lapsley had no doubt as to why he never had a desert sore: 'There was no shortage of onions in the desert and I ate Spanish onions like apples. That's why I never got a desert sore at all.' The preferred treatment was Gentian Violet, but a cream was later produced which had much better results.

Laundering clothing caused a skin problem for one dispatch rider, who was used as a guinea-pig for a petrol-based dry-cleaning process:

> Johnny Kitson was our specialist at inventing things and he decided that he would test me, and he got my underpants and some petrol and he washed the pants in the petrol. They were dry in two minutes and he gave them to me, and I set sail down the road on my motorbike and I ended up with the two legs up on the handlebars because I was roasted with the petrol and there was lead in it so I had to report sick. I went down to the Indian depot and they painted them purple and I had to come back like that, and the boys all admired my purple legs. That's a fact!

> **Gunner Jim Dinsmore**

Two-Five Battery was constantly at the mercy of the desert, the Germans never far away. At the end of August 1941 the men were to be relieved, since they were so exhausted, but the shortage of heavy anti-aircraft defences meant that they were sent to Barrani again in September where they narrowly escaped capture, as the Germans attacked through the Halfaya Pass and also from the south. Because of the strength of the advancing German columns, the army commanders decided to withdraw from the Barrani position, and 25 Battery was forced to retreat.

Jim Dinsmore was returning on his motorcycle to his unit's position at Barrani when he began to meet troops coming towards him, some of whom made it very clear that he was heading in the wrong direction. Then:

> When I got up [to my own camp] I was told we were waiting on the

[code] word BICYCLE, because we were going to evacuate, and next thing I went over and Sinclair – that was the cook – and all were getting ready to move out, and he had three graves that he was over looking at. Well, that was all right. We all got out and got down the line anyway.

George Lapsley has very clear memories of that particular retreat, especially of the reaction of Australian infantrymen to the sight of the gunners pulling out from their front-line positions. Because the battery needed to borrow vehicles, their guns had to be moved out earlier than those of other units, who could simply hitch up their transport and move. Two-Five Battery's lorries would also have to return to collect remaining pieces of equipment. This was lost on the Australians, however, who were moving up: 'and they gave us, well I wouldn't like to repeat what they were calling us. They were roaring, "You Pommy Bastards!" They thought we were running away and they were going up to stop the gap.'

We had a radio location [radar] set on the site and the demolition charge was placed under it; I think, as a matter of fact, that it was there practically all of the time. The chappies that worked this set were dead scared in case it got hit by a stray bullet or something and put off the charge of guncotton. We got the order to move, but we'd no transport, absolutely none, so we had to wait on transport arriving.

And I think it was in the dark that we made the move out of our position in Barrani. As a matter of fact, we weren't even allowed to pull down our tents; I had a wee tent, a bivvy tent, dug into the ground. We had to leave [it] all behind. And we passed the battery headquarters on the way down, and I can distinctly remember they had confiscated my camera a long time previously.

Gunner John Ormsby

The camera had been confiscated in Port Sudan in 1940. John Ormsby realised that the abandoned boxes he could see belonged to his battery headquarters, as they all bore the stencilled numerals 2021, his regiment's tactical number. So he dashed into HQ and found three cameras: 'I put them under my shirt and headed back and I got them distributed to the right men. I got my own and two others. They never were mentioned afterwards by anybody.'

The battery pulled back to Kilo 44 on the Matruh Road and remained there in a state of limbo, prepared to defend itself against air attack. The men realised that fortune had been on their side, for they had narrowly escaped from a closing trap, but they were even luckier than they believed at the time as the advancing Germans had been unable to close the trap. The force attacking through the Halfaya Pass had intended to meet up with an armoured force advancing on Barrani from the south, but this southern arm of the German pincer movement had retreated when the Desert Air Force, whom 25 Battery had been doing such a good job of protecting on the ground, had destroyed their fuel tankers, leaving the panzers with insufficient range to finish the job allocated to them. And so, within twenty-four hours of leaving their positions at Barrani, the battery returned.

Arriving back at Barrani, Jim Dinsmore found out what Davy Sinclair had really buried in the three hastily dug graves. 'It was his beer he had been burying!' But Sinclair's beer was not all that had been interred at Barrani; some members of the battery had also taken the time to conceal the property of an army chaplain, which was restored to him when the positions were re-occupied.

That retreat was 25 Battery's last major action in the desert in 1941, although the day after their return to Barrani they shot down a German bomber. Some time later, the promise to relieve them was finally honoured and they moved to the Nile Delta for their long-awaited rest, before moving into gun positions in the Alexandria defences with the remainder of their regiment.

The North African campaign continued to see-saw until July 1942 when General Auchinleck stopped Rommel at the El Alamein line. From there, in October 1942, General Montgomery launched the offensive that began the collapse of the Axis forces in the region.

With the invasion of French North-West Africa in November 1942 the Germans had to fight on two fronts. After January 1943 the war moved completely into Tunisia, where, following bitter fighting that included the Irish Brigade, German and Italian troops in North Africa surrendered. On 12 May 1943, General Alexander was able to report to Winston Churchill that all enemy opposition had ceased in Africa.

The Sandhills of Mersa Matruh

When 25 Battery moved up the desert for the second time, they quickly produced a battery anthem, 'The Sandhills of Mersa Matruh', written by Derryman **John McLaughlin** (known as Abdul because of his fluency in Arabic) and put to music, using the tune of 'The Green Grassy Slopes of the Boyne', by **George Lapsley**. The song reflects the defiant spirit of those men, so far from home at a very bleak time in the war.

You may talk about your barracks at Mustapha
Or your camps at Mex and Sidi Bishr too,
But my song is of the Western Desert
And the sandhills of Mersa Matruh.

Just take a train at Sidi Gabr station
And travel twelve hours into the blue,
When you hear the sound of bombing and artillery
Then you're getting close to Mersa Matruh.

The Italians assembled at Barrani
Intent for to Alex to break through,
But their armies were soon annihilated
By the wild men of Mersa Matruh.

Now, you Germans who've conquered all Europe
Take this advice I'm giving to you,
Your mothers are waiting back in Berlin
Only death waits at Mersa Matruh.

I'm dreaming tonight of old Ireland
And moonlit nights I've spent with you,
But I'm brought back to earth with Action Stations
And I wake up in Mersa Matruh.

My song is now nearing completion
And I must bid my farewell to you,
So, if you want to join an army, join the Home Guard
And you won't be sent to Mersa Matruh.

The efforts of men like Abdul McLaughlin and George Lapsley were instrumental in sustaining the morale of their comrades in those dark days of early 1941, when Germany was winning everywhere and only the tiny British army in North Africa seemed to be able to stop them.

4
Italy

We were told to hold that crossroads at all costs.

BEFORE the North African campaign had ended, Russia was pressuring the Western Allies to open a Second Front in Europe. Churchill declared that Britain had already been fighting on a second front – North Africa – but this did not satisfy the Soviets who wanted the war taken to mainland Europe. The Americans hoped to invade France in 1943, but were persuaded by Churchill that an attack through Italy, the 'soft under-belly' of Europe as he described it, was more practicable at that time. Thus, on 10 July 1943 Allied troops invaded Sicily in Operation HUSKY, taking the island in a short, sharp campaign. The next phase of Allied strategy was to invade Italy itself.

The large Allied armies in North Africa made this a rational proposition. The attraction was the possibility of a swift campaign taking the Allies through Italy and perhaps into Austria. From there they could attack into Germany itself, which they hoped to reach before the Russians, thus preventing a possible Soviet domination of post-war Europe.

But 'soft under-belly' Italy was not – as the men of the Allied Fifth Army discovered when they landed at Salerno on 9 September 1943 in Operation AVALANCHE. This army, half-American and half-British, was quickly counter-attacked by powerful German forces. At one stage, 6th US Corps was almost forced back into the sea, and as the situation became more desperate every available soldier was thrown into the line to stop the Germans. When 9th (Londonderry) Heavy Anti-Aircraft Regiment landed on the night of 15 September they were soon converted to infantry:

> So we went in that night and . . . when we got there they asked us
> who we were, and we said we were artillery, and they said that was

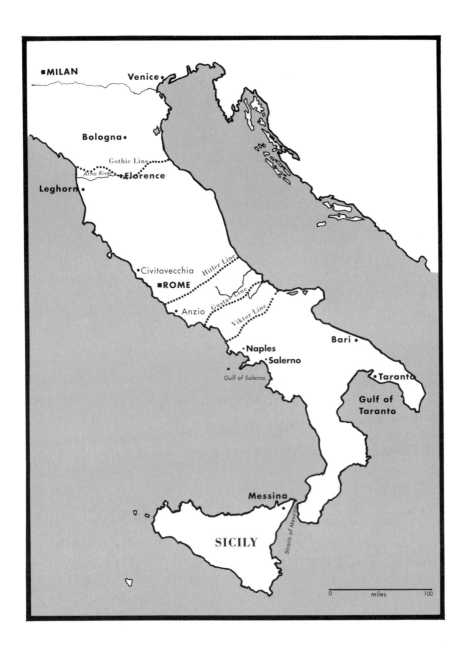

MILAN

Venice

Bologna

Gothic Line

Arno River Florence

Leghorn

Civitavecchia

Hitler Line

ROME

Gustav Line

Anzio

Viktor Line

Bari

Naples

Salerno

Gulf of Salerno

Taranto

Gulf of Taranto

Messina

SICILY

Straits of Messina

0   miles   100

no good for they wanted infantrymen to go up to the front. We lay on the beach and the whistles . . . went. Well, they always talk about the pen being mightier than the sword; we were made infantrymen just at the stroke of a pen, and up we went up to the front line at 3.00 or 4.00 in the morning.

We went up to a place called Tobacco Row and . . . [got] into two old sheds and bedded down until we could see where we were in the morning. When we got up in the morning and had a look around us, there they were: the Germans were in one field and we were in the next. I can tell you now we weren't long getting back. That was my first carry-on as an infantryman, for I wasn't trained to it nor [were] any of the boys. There was some old ex-regular soldiers there right enough, but we weren't right for fighting the Germans at that time as infantry . . . we retired down the line a bit anyway and regrouped.

Bombardier Robert Hamilton, 24 Heavy Anti-Aircraft Battery,
9th (Londonderry) HAA Regiment

A lot of the boys hadn't a clue what was happening. We were just handed a rifle and so many rounds of ammunition. I remember one particular instance . . . . There was a chap handed a box of Bren-gun magazines, and of course he threw it up on his shoulder. It opened and as he walked up the road, cursing and swearing, what amused everybody . . . was an officer coming behind picking up all these magazines. As he was walking along, the magazines were falling out, and there he was trailing on and giving off to the hour! 'It's only a mile they said,' he was grumbling, 'it's more like five miles!' We nicknamed it the Yankee Mile.

When we got up and went into these two old buildings, there was . . . [something] like trestles up, and we posted look-outs for observation but we hadn't a clue what we were doing . . . [in the morning] we went out. It was decided to send a patrol out and I went out with some of the chaps, and this bank, as we would call it, we went down along that, and the first thing I heard was the rattle of a machine-gun. Everybody dived, and I'm sure my impression is still on that bank after all these years – I couldn't get down quick enough.

Sergeant John Taylor, 24 Heavy Anti-Aircraft Battery

The Jerries broke the American line and they were pushed back, and

AVALANCHE! Soldiers of the Allied Fifth Army come ashore on the Salerno
beaches from a Landing Ship Tank (LST) in September 1943 in Operation
AVALANCHE. It was from LSTs like this that the men of 9th (Londonderry) Regiment
disembarked.

the Brigade of Guards had to take over, and we were told they had 4,000 casualties the first night before they formed the line and stabilised it . . . . I was sent up to hold a cross-roads. I had a bombardier and five men and we were told to hold that cross-roads at all costs. One of the boys said to me, 'What do we do if the tanks come down?' I said we'd have to wait for further orders for that one. 'The best thing I could do,' he said, 'is to shout Heil Hitler and join them!'

. . . later on that day there was a crowd of boys . . . getting a bit bored and they had a football and they were out playing football, and the Jerries, we were told, were less than half a mile up the road. This RA [Royal Artillery] officer came along and thought we were madmen. 'Pop' Lapsley said to him, 'don't worry, sir, we'll not touch them.' They said afterwards that it was the boys playing football [that] scared the Jerries! They thought there were a few million people down there and they wouldn't advance.

. . . when we were told to hold the cross-roads, well, we didn't know what to do. I had a tommy-gun and the rest had rifles, three-o-threes. What good's that, Lee-Enfields against tanks? But there was a battery of twenty-five pounders just to the left of us, and I took a walk down to it. There was an officer there and he said, 'Don't worry, we'll stop anything that comes down here.' I was a bit apprehensive about that. I didn't think he could stop the tanks coming down the road.

Well, just at dawn, two tanks broke through and came down and, do you know, I thought that was a brave man. He waited until they were about a hundred yards away before he opened fire and he just stopped them in their tracks. There was no more breakthrough that morning at all. That finished it.

*Sergeant **Jim Canning**, 25 Heavy Anti-Aircraft Battery*

The regiment remained as infantrymen for three days until reinforcements arrived at Salerno; in the meantime Eighth Army moved north from its landing points at the toe of Italy and its heel, Taranto. The Irish Brigade, which had already taken part in the Tunisian and Sicilian campaigns, had yet to be committed to Italy, but a few days after the landings they crossed the Straits of Messina to Italy and moved up to Barletta on the east coast. Since the terrain beyond the Foggia plain was very rough, a seaborne operation was launched, moving the brigade from Barletta along the coast to Termoli, where they were engaged in bitter fighting but succeeded in securing the town against an attack by a German Panzer division.

The Irish Brigade was made up of 6th Royal Inniskilling Fusiliers, 1st Royal Irish Fusiliers and 2nd London Irish Rifles. In fact, the Italian campaign involved more Irish soldiers than any other in the war, for not only were the units of the Irish Brigade and 9th (Londonderry) Regiment included, but also, 1st Irish Guards, 2nd Royal Inniskilling Fusiliers, 1st London Irish Rifles and, from April 1944, the North Irish Horse. On top of this was 117th Light Anti-Aircraft Regiment, which was really 8th Royal Ulster Rifles under another name, as well as 66th Light Anti-Aircraft Regiment, which had also been raised in Northern Ireland.

The arrival of reinforcements at Salerno allowed 9th Regiment to return to artillery duties:

> Seventh Armoured Div[ision] came up and we were called to a sort of a conference at the corner of a field, and I was there and it was a colonel and he said, 'I want you to hold on for twenty-four to thirty-six hours because Monty's coming up with an army *that can fight.*' He said it just like that! And the Americans were listening to this, you see, and that's why he said it – for their benefit. But they [Eighth Army] did, it was about twenty-four hours afterward when they came up, and then we were called back to our guns.
>
> *Sergeant Jim Canning*

> We were ready to go into action anyway against them [the Germans] behind the tanks, and, all of a sudden, it was cancelled. So we looked down the field and there Montgomery was standing with General Mark Clark behind us, and the order then came to get back and get the guns into position. They were going to fire a continuous barrage of shells from *Warspite* [in the Gulf of Salerno].
>
> So we got back in and we had to get alongside big sugar-canes, about ten-feet high, and we pulled in front of the Germans . . . and we started to engage the Jerries there, but in the meantime the barrage was set up from the *Warspite*, and several big heavy ships of the Americans out behind, battleships, and five-fives, four-fives, three-sevens, twenty-five pounders [were used], and for hours and hours we pounded at the Jerry. He was on a height at this time. So, after a couple of hours . . . the infantry made a push in and shifted

Men of 6th Royal Inniskilling Fusiliers in the Irish Brigade on the march in the Mediterranean sun. The Irish Brigade's first action on mainland Italy was at Termoli, on the east coast, in October 1943.

Jerry from the top of Salerno.

Bombardier Robert Hamilton

The bombardment was carried out by a wide range of weaponry, including the 3.7-inch heavy anti-aircraft guns of the Londonderry Regiment. The regiment was engaged in firing at German artillery, in what was known as counter-battery fire. Their fire proved very effective, and although the Germans tried to bombard the Derrymen they were unsuccessful:

> We didn't get one shell hit in our positions at all, but some medium gunners near to us were hit very badly. I think they lost a lot of men, they were hit by some very big stuff. One of our troops [a battery was divided into two four-gun troops] had a lucky escape, some 170s fell across their positions, but nobody was hurt. There were only a couple of people hit at different times by shell splinters, but they weren't [seriously injured]. We were very lucky there.
>
> **Gunner Tommy McCready, 24 Heavy Anti-Aircraft Battery**

After the Salerno breakout, Naples fell in October and the Allies moved towards the Gustav Line, where the Germans had mustered their forces to stop the Allied advance. German forces in Italy were commanded by Field Marshal Albert Kesselring, probably Germany's finest general of the war. It was Kesselring's skill, plus the lack of Allied forces committed to the campaign, that turned Italy into a nightmare for the soldiers of Fifth and Eighth Armies as they fought their way from river valley to river valley. In the severe winter of 1944, the Allies were bogged down in the mountains, advancing only seventy miles in four months.

The name of Monte Cassino sums up the problems of the Italian campaign more than any other. Overlooking the route to Rome, the Germans had turned Monte Cassino and the surrounding mountain-tops into a chain of fortresses. To try to break this deadlock, the Allied air forces later bombed and destroyed the Benedictine monastery on the mountain-top, but the bombing proved worthless; the infantry continued to suffer and die in further attacks on the mountain.

Before the bombing there had been a bold Allied attempt to turn the Cassino position and to break the Gustav Line. To do this, the Allies had launched another seaborne landing in January 1944. Intended to cut the

German forces off, it was part of a two-pronged attack, with a crossing of the Rapido River, to coincide with the landing which took place at Anzio:

[On 22] January we [landed] at Anzio. Of course, we didn't know we were going to Anzio, we were well up the coast before we realised where we were going. So, then they told us we were going in behind the lines to make a landing at Anzio . . . . [That was] when . . . a couple of them blew up with the mines, and what happened actually . . . was [that] the Italian mines were in boxes, in wooden boxes, and the detectors, they couldn't pick them up, you see. So . . . the engineers had to prod the beaches with their bayonets to find these landmines.

So, eventually we did get in . . . the amphibian I was driving, I just got halfway up the beach when a shell landed . . . I noticed the smoke and everything but I didn't know at the time that the amphibian had been hit until I got up onto the beach and went to get instructions as to what to do. I had an artillery piece on and some men, so I wanted to see what I was going to do with this; it had to be lifted off by a crane. And the sergeant said to me, 'Paddy, you'll not go very far, for there's a big hole in the front of your amphibian.' It was about two [feet] or so in diameter. But it didn't stop you. You got another one.

From that beachhead that we landed on, I think it was about three or four days before eventually we moved up into the town of Anzio itself, and that's where we were stationed right up until I got wounded. We went in on 22 January, and I got wounded on 9 March, but we'd some hot days and hot nights in the same beachhead. I think it was about eight-miles long and three- or four-miles deep.

Driver John Logue, *Royal Army Service Corps*

Although the Anzio landing was virtually unopposed, the other prong of the operation, the Rapido River crossing, was a disaster, with 36th (US) Division slaughtered by a smaller, well-dug-in German formation. The deadlock continued and the men on the Anzio beachhead were sentenced to an unknown period of purgatory in a place that came to be known as 'Hell's Half-Acre'.

. . . they told us . . . the troops from Monte Cassino would be through to us in forty-eight hours, that Alexander was going to make a push

A column of DUKWs comes ashore at Anzio. The first vehicle carries a British twenty-five-pounder field gun, but the DUKW crew are American. It was one of these amphibians that John Logue drove throughout the Italian campaign.

The enemy. Soldiers of a German Fallschirmjaeger (Parachute) Regiment study a map as they prepare to oppose a British attack. The Fallschirmjaeger were said by Field Marshal Alexander to be the toughest troops Germany possessed.

along with us, synchronised like, as we landed at Anzio . . . that Eighth Army would put in a big push and they would break through to us in forty-eight hours. But we went in on 22 January, I got wounded on 9 March and they hadn't broken through then.

I went back to hospital. I was flown back to North Africa again, to Tunis. I spent a while . . . outside of Tunis in . . . a field hospital, and then I was taken back to Algiers, and that's where they ended up patching me up . . . . Eventually I got back to my unit again, and they were just on breaking through then. I think that was May sometime. It was a long forty-eight hours!

Driver John Logue

Cassino finally fell in Operation DIADEM in May. Irish soldiers were involved in the final battle, with the Irish Brigade cutting the road to Rome, forcing the Germans to withdraw from the monastery which was then taken by the Polish Corps. There had been many acts of incredible bravery from soldiers of the Irish Brigade. The gallantry of one young soldier of the London Irish Rifles inspired his company commander to recommend him for a posthumous Victoria Cross:

During the attack on Sinagoga farm, my company was held up by a German eighty-eight-millimetre gun . . . concealed behind a haystack. It was causing considerable damage to the tanks that were supporting us. Corporal [Jimmy] Barnes, who came from Keady, saw this. Now, his platoon commander had been very seriously wounded, so Corporal Barnes took his section forward to try to do something about this eighty-eight, which was stopping our tanks [from] getting forward. But one by one his men were cut down by machine-gun fire from their left flank, and then Corporal Barnes was left alone. He went on alone and then he too was shot and fell dead. But the crew of the eighty-eight had abandoned their gun, and our tanks were able to move up. Corporal Barnes was an incredibly brave young man, and after the battle I wrote a VC citation for him. Unfortunately, it was never awarded, and because he'd been killed no other award could be made.

Major Desmond Woods, *MC, 2nd London Irish Rifles*

This action opened the road northward for the Allies. A few days later, the Hitler Line, a fall-back defensive system behind the Gustav Line, was broken. Anzio was relieved, and Rome fell to Fifth Army on 5 June.

We went from Anzio to Civitavecchia, the port of Rome . . . that was a great sensation, going through Rome in the amphibians and everybody out cheering. It was a change. Not that they [the Italian civilians] weren't very good to us all along . . . even when I got wounded I remember very well an old Italian woman coming over and putting oranges and grapes on my chest where I was lying on the stretcher as they carried me up to the ship. And I never forgot that.

Driver John Logue

Friendly relations with the Italian people had also been established by the gunners of 9th (Londonderry) Regiment during their time in Naples. After the breaking of the Gustav Line, they moved to Anzio and then, through Rome, to Civitavecchia. They had pleasant memories of the people of Naples and found that such friendliness continued as they moved up Italy:

We got on very well with the local people . . . we found out . . . they were very ill-fed and poorly clothed, too. And at the time, where we were was . . . a punishment to us because we got lost outside of Naples in the push, and our colonel brought us back and put us in between five carboni dumps and these were lit by the Germans, and we were sitting in the middle, and that's where our gunsite was. At night the Jerry come in over these to raid Naples. Well, that was our punishment for getting lost for two days.

But anyway, the people used to come down there for the carboni and we got on very well with them . . . they had no food and the thing that they really wanted most was salt, because they hadn't seen salt for years and we were able to give them some salt. We said we were from Ireland and they said '*Irlandese*' and then they searched us, looking for the Roman Catholic things round our necks, and we said we had none, we were Protestants. '*Ah, niente Protestante in Irlanda, Irlanda molti-Catholici.*'

We were allowed trips into Rome. These trips were organised by the late Reverend Crooks and a Roman Catholic chaplain, too. We got a trip in to see the Vatican, which is really a lovely place to see, and there we met the Pope and, being a Protestant myself, I was interested

and not interested and I thought I would go ahead anyway, and in we
went with the two clergymen and we met a Londonderry monsignor
there who showed us round and got us a lovely interview with the
Pope, and I received a little medal with a chain from the Pope. So,
when I came back to the camp Willie Ferguson from the Creggan was
there, so I told him about it. I thought he would appreciate the chain
more than I did, so I gave it to him.

Bombardier Robert Hamilton

By now the Luftwaffe, the German air force, had very few planes left, and
because of this 9th Regiment converted to field gunners, supporting the 34th
(US) Division's infantry and tanks in the capture of the port city of Livorno.
In August they moved up to take part in the battles along the River Arno,
where one of their targets could very easily have been the Leaning Tower
of Pisa. However, the High Command had other ideas:

. . . we took a position in facing the Leaning Tower of Pisa. I'd say
we were 400 to 500 yards off it and we got our guns down there, and
there was a smaller battery in front of us, two twenty-five pounders.

But we were very lucky. We pulled into a big farmhouse and . . .
well, our grub wasn't just so good . . . when we went down into the
grounds of it, we found turkeys and ducks and all waiting to be fed,
so we fed them and we also ate them.

But coming to the firing at the Leaning Tower of Pisa, we had to fire
five degrees each side of it and we could see the Germans coming down
inside that five degrees and into the wee river in front of them, and
having a swim and going back up again . . . you had to be dead-on
if you were going to fire on either side, because the big scare was to
save this Leaning Tower of Pisa. I could never get over that. To hell
with the Leaning Tower of Pisa, like, I wouldn't care about it if it had
[fallen] down on top of the Germans.

That's where we were when we got word to come home and . . . at
that time I was a GPO Ack's assistant to Major Laird. And the Don R
came up about 2.00 or 3.00 in the morning, and we wondered what
he was doing at that time of the morning because it was a terrible road
to get up, [as] the Germans were shelling it . . . . Tommy McCready
was the telephonist in the command post, and the first thing that came
over on my head and breast [telephone] set was, 'Hammy! We're going

home!' You know what I said back to him – we'd been listening to that for years, you know. And he said, 'It's true this time', but then Major Laird came on and he said, 'Get the number ones [gun commanders] to the command post', so I got the number ones to the command post and he then instructed them that we were going home, and each gun would pull out separate and make a run for it down the road and over the bridges.

Now, these bridges had a big smokescreen over them all the time, and they were pontoon bridges, five of them together, looped, and . . . once you got over the other side . . . you knew you were going to Derry all right. Up to that you had a chance of getting lifted out [by German shellfire], but anyway number-four gun was to pull out first and number-three gun was to fire forty rounds for them. That meant they were firing eighty, and so forth . . . until it came to number one. Number-one gun, it was to fire and then clear. That left the command post, which I was in then with the predictor and heightfinder and spotter and Major Laird in his jeep.

And number-four gun, I never saw it before, when I happened to look across I could see the flashes coming out and I realised there was something wrong there. You're not supposed to see the flashes there, sure she's down on the ground. So I crept over and up over the top and looked in – he was firing on the wheels, which shouldn't [happen] at all . . . but everybody was anxious to get home, so he was firing and where they went I don't know . . . and once he cleared, then we had to lift the predictor and all into the three-tonner and we made our dash to the other side out of the road. We all got down safe anyway and . . . then we were headed into Rome and then from Rome to Naples and then a ship for home.

Bombardier Robert Hamilton

In early September 1944, the regiment sailed for the UK. John Logue was still making his way up Italy. The Allied advance had slowed down yet again because the Americans had decided to invade the south of France and had withdrawn 150,000 soldiers from Italy. This ended any possibility of finishing the Italian campaign in 1944. Another hard winter's fighting followed in the Apennine mountains.

The Irish Brigade spent most of that winter in mountain positions; towards

Happy Ever After

Driver John Logue had been wounded twice in action, and when the war ended in Italy his superiors offered him a posting which was to leave him with very pleasant memories of the country:

> The commanding officer . . . asked me, 'Would you take a good job in Venice?' And I said, 'Well, sir, I don't know what to do, I'll leave it up to you. I don't like leaving the boys that I've been with all this time from Africa, Sicily and Italy.' . . . But he said, 'You'll not be leaving them. I'm sending you over to the Lido in Venice to look after a vehicle because' – this is what he said to me – 'I have a cowboy over there, and all he thinks of is wine, women and song, and that's no good to me because he's going to get me shot. Instead of Hitler getting me I'll be put up against a post.' So he asked me if I'd take the job and he said, 'All you have to do is look after your vehicle . . . as you've done all along and do the job that I want you to do . . . that company [in Venice] only [gives] you a bed, [gives] you your food, [but] we pay you and you're with us all the time.'

John Logue accepted the offer. In Venice he was given the job of transporting civilian labour to and from prisoner-of-war camps. One of those civilians was a young Italian woman, Edera Santin, who was to become his wife. However, the marriage very nearly did not transpire because of a remark she made one evening on an ancient bridge overlooking the Venetian canals:

> *'Do vedi a domani a le due e mezza a spiaggi.'* I said to myself, 'Paddy, I know what it is. She means she'll meet you tomorrow at 2.30 pm for a feed of spaghetti.' But . . . what she did really say was, 'I'll see you tomorrow down at the beach' – the *'spiaggi'* . . . . So, if I didn't learn the hard way I don't know who did.
> So I went down on Sunday at 2.30 pm. I left the camp early.

I had a fifty tin of cigarettes and a couple of bars of army hard chocolate. You were only supposed to take a wee piece off it [at a time] . . . but I used to give it to them and they lapped it [up]. It's a wonder they didn't snuff it. But anyhow, I landed down at this bridge . . . . I thought to myself, 'She's going to pick me up at 2.30 pm now for this feed of spaghetti.'

Well, I went there . . . and I had every cigarette in my possession smoked at 8.30 at night and I was still sitting there, and every blade of grass round me ate, whenever she came up the street, her and her squad, and she was . . . I could hear the chitters and capers of her coming up, 'Da-da-da-da-da-la-la-la-bah'. So I tried to calm her down as best I could . . . and we went for a walk, the whole lot of us, and she took me behind the village, which was only ten minutes from where I was sitting, to the beach where I should have met her at 2.30 pm!

Driver John Logue and Edera Santin after their wedding. The bride's coat was made from a dyed army blanket. John Logue wears the ribbons of his campaign medals and stars; the two stripes above his left cuff are wound-stripes and the badge under his shoulder is that of a commando Beach Group.

the end of the winter, however, they moved into the line along the River Senio. The situation there was similar to the Western Front in the First World War, with opposing forces in trenches that, at times, were only yards apart. Trench raids and mortaring were common features of life along the Senio, but in April the brigade was involved in the final break-out, with the London Irish mounted in armoured personnel carriers, called Kangaroos, supported by tanks and by infantry, including the other two battalions of the brigade. The 'Kangaroo Army' played an important part in that breakthrough and in the final collapse of German resistance in northern Italy.

The war in Italy ended on 2 May 1945 when Field Marshal Alexander took the surrender of all German forces in Italy and Austria, just six days before VE Day. The Italian campaign had been a hard slog for the ordinary soldier.

5

North-West Europe, 1944–45

They got about halfway across a large open space and got massacred.

ON 6 June 1944, D-Day, Allied armies under General Bernard Montgomery, the victor of El Alamein, landed on the Normandy beaches to begin the final campaign of the war in Europe and to end German domination of the continent.

Not all the troops of the Allied Liberation armies went into France by sea. Some had parachuted in the night before and others went in by glider on D-Day. Among those glider troops were 1st Royal Ulster Rifles, whose flight began at Brize Norton in Oxfordshire:

> The gliders were very lightly made. The first ones we had, the small Hotspurs, they only held about nine or ten people. If you hit anything hard they just fell apart, which saved you a lot of injuries. It was always said that you could read the cricket scores on the inside of the wings from the paper. The ones we went to Normandy in were the bigger type, which held a complete platoon and all their equipment.
>
> The flight was very uneventful, very calm, until we got over the fleet . . . we had support from the HMS *Arethusa*. Well, just as we flew over, it let off a broadside and the gliders went about a hundred feet up in the air and then down again, which was very disturbing. Then it got a wee bit rough. There was some 'ack-ack', and there was some turbulence, and a lot of people were sick, probably a bit of nerves as well as the aircraft.
>
> But the landing was as cushy as we'd ever had a landing. The Germans, well, I don't suppose they knew where we were landing, but the places where gliders were liable to land, they had spiked them with big stakes about nine-feet high . . . which were supposed to impede the

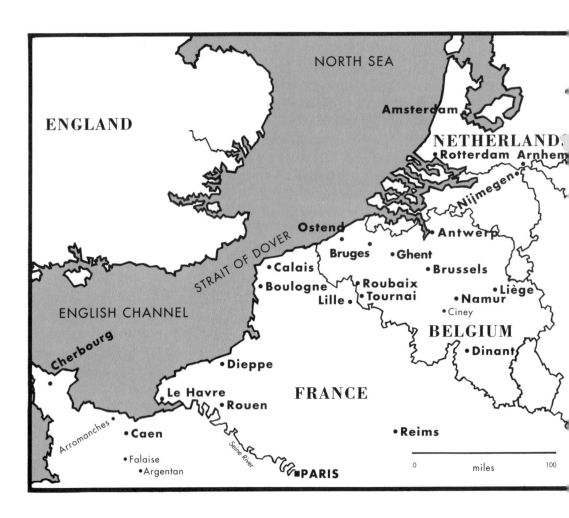

gliders. But we landed safely. I think we had only about two casualties in the whole battalion.

Major Jack Chapman, 1st Royal Ulster Rifles

The airborne troops were to secure areas behind the beaches, including the bridges across the River Orne, to prevent German reinforcements from moving up to the beachhead. The job of 1st Royal Ulster Rifles was to capture and hold two villages, Longueval and Sainte Honorine. They had been told that this would be a relatively straightforward action, but the estimates of German troops in the area had been wrong. The presence of sizeable German units training in the area had not been foreseen, and these units were thrown into action with devastating effect by Field Marshal Rommel, who was commanding the defences of France:

> We then were pinned in and spent probably a week trying to get out, and being driven back, doing patrols at night, which were a bit dicey, and being sniped and mortared at the same time. We had various attempts at Sainte Honorine and each time we were hammered. We got a lot of casualties from there.
>
> The powers-that-be decided that some of the other battalions . . . would come through us and take Sainte Honorine. We cleared the start-line without any bother, they took over and we got back. I got hit on the way back, and most of my platoon was wiped out. And they [the other troops] got about halfway across a large open space and got massacred themselves.
>
> . . . airborne forces were very lightly armed. We'd nothing heavy with us, and if you had tanks against you, you hadn't a hope in hell, really.

Major Jack Chapman

The Rifles were eventually relieved by infantrymen from the main invasion force, which had come across by sea. As well as the problems caused by the German troops who were in the area by chance, the German coast defences at Omaha and Utah beaches, where the American army was going ashore, threatened to push General Bradley's forces back into the sea. The British and Canadian armies had to assist their allies; it was then that the wisdom of appointing the experienced Montgomery, a proven battlefield commander, to command all the invasion troops became clear.

Even after the break-out from the beachhead, the Normandy countryside provided the Germans with a strong ally. Ditches and hedges were natural obstacles for tanks and gave defenders plenty of cover. The Allies became bogged down in what was known as the Battle of Normandy, and more troops had to be poured in, among them the men of 6 Light Anti-Aircraft Battery from Coleraine, who were marooned when their landing craft tried to get them to the beachhead:

> At the time . . . that we landed my impression was of coming down the nets into the DUKWs, loaded like a pack mule . . . if you fell in you never would have come up again . . . plus the fact that when we got over near the shore the tide had turned and we had to lie until the tide come back in again.
>
> *Sergeant Bob Balmer, 6 Light Anti-Aircraft Battery*

> The sea was very rough at the time and I remember . . . when we couldn't get landing I thought to myself, 'They'll blow us out of the water', because we were really sitting-ducks. I think the feeling generally was: 'Let's get to hell out of here and get onto the beach' . . . because the longer we sat the longer they could get targeted on us.
>
> *Lance Bombardier Sam Anderson, 6 Light Anti-Aircraft Battery*

> . . . having got so far and all keyed up, ready to go ashore and then to be stopped because the tide was out . . . well, the longer we waited the worse the tension was, and then we started to get worried. A minute seemed an hour, and we were all the time wondering just what was going to come . . . and have a go at us, and the nerves were getting very, very frayed. It was a great relief when the tide came in and we were able to get ashore.
>
> *Lieutenant Dick Gage, 6 Light Anti-Aircraft Battery*

> We landed at a place they called Arromanches and then we went on up the road and on to Bayeux. But from [where] we landed at Arromanches, going up for about a mile, or a couple of miles, there was a terrible lot of dead belonging to the Hampshire Regiment, just lying along the road . . . young lads. And some of the bodies had turned black, they'd been lying so long.
>
> *Sergeant Bob Balmer*

From Bayeux 6 Light Anti-Aircraft Battery moved on towards Caen, the next major objective for the Allies. Caen fell on 9 July after a series of bloody battles, and the first soldiers to enter the city were men of 2nd Royal Ulster Rifles.

The Battle of Normandy continued until 20 August with some of the fiercest fighting of the war. German resistance was so strong that the advance took longer than planned; their mortar fire was so heavy and caused so many casualties that unusual measures had to be taken: the Coleraine battery, for example, swopped its anti-aircraft guns for tanks:

> I couldn't really believe it because I thought, 'Well, someone's having us on again.' We'd . . . had all this training on Bofors and to be suddenly told we were going to go into tanks just didn't seem on at all. We didn't mind . . . we'd heard about the cavalry going over into mechanised transport, but never in the wide world did we think we were going to be, what, cooped up in sardine-tins. And that's what they were. When we were out in the open and the Bofors went off, that wasn't too bad, but being inside a tank . . . it wasn't just on for us at all.
>
> *Lieutenant Dick Gage*

> Tank personnel took us up at night and then they left us. None of us had any idea of how to drive a tank. If the Germans came we were sitting-ducks. Two men had to stay all night with the things, and one particular night, where we were in a small orchard, Sergeant Hunter and me . . . built an air-raid shelter, but the mortars were that heavy [that] I left him and I went into the tank and slept.
>
> The next morning a lot of top-brass came up and we told them – we were in a hollow – not to go up to the top of the bank. They wouldn't listen to us and up they went. They weren't right up until they were getting shelled and mortared all over the place, running and trying to get into the tanks with us.
>
> *Sergeant Bob Balmer*

> I thought to myself, 'What am I doing here anyhow? I should have another badge on me, a tank badge instead of an artillery badge, same as Monty had.' He wore two badges . . . I think they [the tanks]

The price of war. The destruction in the Falaise Gap is shown in this photograph. As late as 1944 the German army was still using large numbers of horses as transport, and inevitably these unfortunate animals were added to the toll of suffering in the battle for Normandy.

were practically obsolete at the time that we took these things over. I thought to myself, 'Do they want us to create miracles with these things?' They didn't give us very much time, you know, to learn the tanks after coming off a Bofors gun; it was an entirely different kettle of fish altogether.

Lance Bombardier Sam Anderson

These tanks were just old things that had been given to us, and in order to get the right elevation . . . we had to . . . dig down below it, or if we wanted to get another range we had to . . . jack it up and put planks underneath it. Really, when I say Fred Karno, he wasn't in it at all, he was in a different lot to us.

Lieutenant Dick Gage

When the barrage started there was the boy who fired the gun, the boy that was laying for elevation and myself, and of course we knew nothing about tanks, and I was sitting with my head out of the edge of the turret when the first shells went off and it wasn't very long until I had the turret closed. The noise was damnable.

. . . then . . . we decided, because there were no drivers we would try and learn to drive these tanks ourselves, in case we had to get out of the road. Sergeant Campbell got in one day in an orchard and before he was finished there wasn't an appletree standing, he knocked every appletree in the place down. But we thought we'd be as well to try and learn to drive them anyway, in case we had to get out of the road.

Sergeant Bob Balmer

The break-out from Normandy took place when the British and Canadian armies lured the strongest part of the German army into the area of the Falaise Gap. General Patton's Third US Army was then able to strike out towards Brittany and the west coast of France. The aim was to capture the French ports from where the Germans were operating their U-boats. The operation at the Falaise Gap was one of the most horrific episodes in the Battle for Normandy:

I'll never forget the Falaise Gap. As we went through it, at each side of the road there were bodies piled up. You'd [have] thought it was [like] . . . you know, the way you pile up sheafs of corn. There was dead bodies piled up, horses . . . there was a terrible stench from the dead bodies. That was one thing I'll never forget about the Falaise Gap. I would say there was as many dead Germans as there was British . . . to my memory. The barrage was very heavy and we thought [if] we couldn't drive the tanks, we were stuck there. If the Germans had broken out and [had come] towards us we'd [have] had it, that was it.

Lance Bombardier Sam Anderson

. . . when all was going on you didn't have time to think what was going to happen to you, and things like that. You had a job to do and you intended to get that job done. It was upsetting to see that the burial parties of either side hadn't had time, because of the battle, to get out and do any burying. That was upsetting, but, as I say, the thing is that with the heat of the moment and all that was going on, terrible thing to say, you put that in the background. All you wanted to do was [to] get on and get the job done. It wasn't until afterwards, when things quietened down, that it really hit you and you just realised how near you [had come] to being one of those that was alongside the road. Horrible thoughts, and really things . . . one tends to try and forget. All you want to do now . . . is remember the happier sides and not those really terrifying bits. And they were terrifying bits, we realised that when it was quiet.

Lieutenant Dick Gage

After the horror of the Falaise Gap, the battery took part in Second British Army's dash through northern France into Belgium, where they entered Brussels just after its liberation by the Guards' Armoured Division, led by the Irish Group and made up of an armoured battalion and a mobile infantry battalion of the Irish Guards.

After Brussels, 6 Light Anti-Aircraft Battery's next major job was Operation MARKET GARDEN, now remembered for 1st Airborne Division's unsuccessful drop on the bridge at Arnhem. Earlier, some of the gunners had the experience of serving along the Dutch-Belgian border in armoured cars:

We were with a brigadier and he fancied himself as Montgomery, and you had to go where this old fool wanted to go. We were stationed at Bourg Leopold and . . . this madman always wanted to be up in the thick of the thing. But he ran into a German artillery barrage one day

Objective taken! Soldiers of 1st Royal Ulster Rifles, who had earlier landed by
glider, dig in along the River Issel after reaching their objective.

Coleraine gunners of 6 Light Anti-Aircraft Battery with a forty-millimetre Bofors
gun. This photograph was taken earlier in the war when the battery was in Egypt.

and he wasn't so brave . . . he couldn't get the armoured car turned quick enough to get out of the road.

Sergeant Bob Balmer

While the airborne army was dropping on the bridges along the road to Arnhem, General Horrocks's 30 Corps was dashing up that road to relieve the airborne soldiers. At the front of that dash along Hell's Highway were the Irish Guards and 6 Light Anti-Aircraft Battery in a column; their front line was only the width of a single tank, a tempting target for the German Panzer divisions along the way.

In Holland it was one road more or less that the army was trying to get up, and each side of the road was muck and dirt to the eyes. We were pushing on to get to Grave and we were stopped at Veghel and we were there that night, and the Germans came in round the back.

Sergeant Bob Balmer

We were very relieved to be back on the 'ack-ack' again and we were mainly doing defence of the bridges and that sort of thing. But when we had been told that the Panzers were in the locality, it was worrying because we were not very sure, as war was, whether we were really going to break out. We kept our fingers crossed and hoped for the best, and fortunately it came off and we were able to get clear.

Lieutenant Dick Gage

I think really what happened was we were actually moving too fast . . . we were making too much progress and this is why we nearly got surrounded . . . the German pincer movement, we nearly got caught up in it but, luckily enough, we got the length of Nijmegen . . . one thing that sticks out in my memory was the [sight of] paratroopers coming over. Now, I think they were in old Dakotas . . . they were getting shot up all over the place. You could see nothing, only Dakotas coming out of the sky.

Lance Bombardier Sam Anderson

Ever since Normandy, the ground forces had had the support of the Allied Tactical air forces, which proved essential in the advance through France and Belgium. A tank commander or an infantry officer could call on the help of Typhoon fighter-bombers to knock out enemy positions, and in a matter of minutes his call was answered:

> They were terrific. They came down after the German eighty-eight-
> millimetre guns, and when you seen them coming you had an idea
> they would shift the eighty-eight-millimetres. They went right down,
> you'd have thought they were going to go into the gun before they let
> go. They were the bravest men I've ever seen.
>
> *Sergeant Bob Balmer*

It was Christmas before the battery was again involved in a major action.
Two German armies had broken the American line in the Ardennes, and
British forces, including the Ulster Rifles and the Coleraine gunners, were
sent in to retrieve the situation. Montgomery's men met the Germans in
conditions bordering on the Arctic:

> We were in a big convent school for one night when we were drafted up
> the Ardennes, which was a terrible place, with frost and snow. Thank
> God we weren't that long in it. We went back down through Namur,
> down into Belgium again. That was bloody awful, we were frozen. I
> remember on Old Year's night we were taking shelter in a house and
> the old Belgian bloke told us the big stove was 'good heat, good heat'.
> In the morning there was damn-all in it, only the front of the thing was
> rusted, but we thought it was a flame and we were frozen.
>
> *Sergeant Bob Balmer*

In spite of such conditions the Battle of the Bulge, the fight for the Ardennes,
was won by the Allies, who resumed their advance towards Germany at the
end of January 1945.

The Rhine was crossed in Operation PLUNDER in March, and among
the first units across that river were 1st Royal Ulster Rifles and 6 Light
Anti-Aircraft Battery. The Coleraine men were involved in final operations
in Germany before Field Marshal Montgomery accepted the surrender of
Hitler's forces in May.

By then the world had begun to learn of the horrors of the concentration
camps. Footage of the scenes at the liberation of Belsen had been shown
across the globe, but the gunners from Coleraine found their own horror

when they were sent to guard German PoWs in what had been a death camp for its earlier Russian inmates.

> We knew well beforehand when we were coming near these burial pits, as we called them. If the wind was blowing towards you it really was awful. And then when you came and saw it, well, words can't describe it. I leave it to yourself . . . what one really comes to when you see . . . a trench with bodies thrown in just anyhow.
>
> *Lieutenant Dick Gage*

> The way they disposed of the bodies was they put a digger in and dug a great big deep trench and just buried them in it. But you could've smelt the stench of bodies half a mile away. It was terrible, a terrible experience to come across.
>
> *Lance Bombardier Sam Anderson*

> You come to this large hole that had been bulldozed out and then you see, looking in, just a mass of twisted bodies thrown in, one on top of the other. You wanted to tear yourself away, you wanted to do something, but there was nothing you could do for them. The only thing to do was go away; and, well, it upset you for a very long time afterwards.
>
> *Lieutenant Dick Gage*

> They were a very arrogant crowd of prisoners, the German prisoners. They'd march out into the moss every morning cutting peat. They always went down singing German songs, a very arrogant crowd.
>
> *Sergeant Bob Balmer*

> You felt like just lining them up and mowing them down. Not all Germans were bad, it was the Nazis, the SS and people like that. The ordinary German people themselves were all right.
>
> *Lance Bombardier Sam Anderson*

> Well, the Russians weren't all that great either, because one night Sergeant Dunlop and me were out [on] a walk and coming up to this wee house we heard this terrible squealing and shouting. In those days you carried guns with you, and we went into the house,

First in, Last Out

'First in, last out' has long been the unofficial motto of the Royal Engineers, signifying the importance of their combat roles, from clearing paths through minefields to building bridges under fire. Typical of such tasks was one given to an Ulster squadron, who were dropped behind the German defences on 6 June 1944.

The squadron was 591 (Antrim) Parachute Squadron, RE, which earlier, as the Antrim Fortress Company, had been one of the first two Territorial Army units created in Northern Ireland in 1937. It became 591 (Antrim) Field Company in 1940, converting to the parachute role in May 1943.

Shortly after midnight on the night of 5 June 1944, 1 and 3 Troops of 591 Squadron were dropped east of the Orne bridge to clear a landing zone for gliders of 6th Airborne Division, who were to land at 3.30 am. This they did speedily and successfully before turning their hands to mine-clearing and reconnoitring of routes from the landing zone; they also laid a minefield to strengthen the positions to be held by glider troops.

At the same time, 2 Troop had been dropped near the heavy gun battery at Merville. Unfortunately, the drop was inaccurate, and few of the Antrim sappers reached the battery. It was, however, put out of action. The sappers then joined and fought with other units until 591 Squadron reassembled. The squadron stayed in France until August, when they returned to the UK. They were later rushed to the Ardennes as part of 6th Airborne Division, to stop the German offensive that winter, and subsequently took part in the Rhine crossing.

and these Russians had this old man and woman lined up against the wall, trying to get whatever belongings they had: clothes and money and jewellery. Luckily enough, we were able to dispatch them out of the road, but if we hadn't [have] been there the old folk were due for a beating-up. Course you couldn't in a way fault them because [the Russians] had suffered a terrible lot. But it was a bad way to take it out on old people.

Sergeant Bob Balmer

The thing is that with the Germans and the Russians, the feeling towards them is, well, I suppose, at the risk of upsetting people, there was the animal instinct that was in us all. It was just, well, it's either you or me, and I think that was war. It's brought back a lot of memories . . . memories that I want to forget, very quickly . . . very quickly.

Lieutenant Dick Gage

Between D-Day and VE Day, over 500,000 Allied soldiers had been killed, wounded or captured in the final year of the war. There is a belief that it was almost a triumphal procession through Europe for the men of the British, Canadian, American and French armies, but the war graves which mark the line of their advance tell another story:

I went back on the fortieth anniversary and people had said, 'That's a great mistake, you'll think of the fellas you left there.' I was quite sure it wouldn't. The only thing that upset me, I think, was to go round the cemeteries there where a lot of people you knew were and to realise how terribly young they were. At the time you didn't think you were young. You were in your twenties, you were pretty old, but in actual fact they were boys . . . . at a place called Merville there was a very big gun battery and a great friend of mine, an Ulster Rifleman, was in that and he was killed at it. And in the battery now they have pictures of everybody who was killed, and there was Mike and to see him so young shocked me. I hadn't realised quite what it was.

Major Jack Chapman

6
Burma

We believed we were the elite, that's what kept us going.

T HE men who fought in Burma called themselves the Forgotten Army, and although the Burma conflict was the longest land campaign of the Second World War it is now the one about which least is known.

The Japanese attack on Pearl Harbour on 7 December 1941 was one of a series of attacks in the Far East. That same day Japanese aircraft bombed Singapore, their ground forces invaded Thailand and Malaya and the following day their troops invaded Hong Kong, Guam, Wake Island and the Phillipines. On 10 December the battleships HMS *Repulse* and HMS *Prince of Wales* were sunk off Malaya; five days later Allied troops in Malaya and Burma were on the retreat.

By mid February the Japanese were pushing British and Indian forces back rapidly in Burma and had attacked the Australian mainland. So dangerous was the situation in Burma that Winston Churchill sent General Harold Alexander there to get as much of the army as possible out of the country and into India. In May 1942 the last of Alexander's troops crossed the border into India. Among the survivors of that retreat were men of 1st Royal Inniskilling Fusiliers; they had suffered heavy losses and only a hundred men from their original strength reached India. Reinforcements were sent out to strengthen the frontier defences and to prepare for a counter-attack against the Japanese. Among these reinforcements was 8th (Belfast) Heavy Anti-Aircraft Regiment.

Belfast gunners were employed as both field and anti-aircraft artillery when they moved as part of the force that went into the Arakan on Burma's north-west coast. This region was the rice garden of India, and the gunners found themselves having to build gun positions in completely unfamiliar conditions:

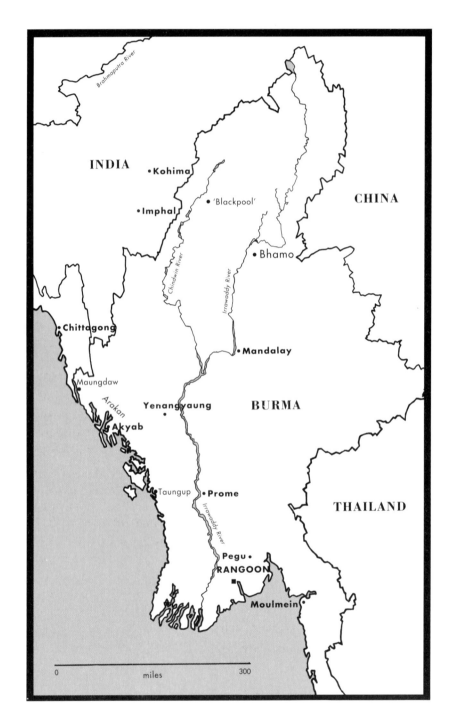

INDIA

•Kohima

•Imphal

•'Blackpool'

CHINA

•Bhamo

Chindwin River

Irrawaddy River

•Chittagong

•Mandalay

Maungdaw

Arakan

•Yenangyaung

BURMA

•Akyab

Taungup

•Prome

Irrawaddy River

THAILAND

Pegu•

RANGOON
■

Moulmein•

Brahmapura River

0   miles   300

When the guns went off, if we'd gone down any length at all the guns would have disappeared into water, so we had to build up on the hard paddy.

Captain Harry Porter, 22 Heavy Anti-Aircraft Battery

. . . they employed coolies, who dug a vast hole in the ground and what they took out of that they threw up into a mound, flattened it out and then the guns were set on top of that, so that when the monsoon did come they were completely surrounded by water except these four or five small islands with guns sitting on top of them.

Sergeant Cunningham Fowler, 23 Heavy Anti-Aircraft Battery

Once the monsoon started the roads just disappeared, and it became a complete sea of mud. We must have filled millions of sandbags, and in the heat and humidity it wasn't easy work. We moved quite a lot because you had to move once you were spotted. The Japanese air force had supremacy in those days; in fact, they had it for two years, so our job was to keep them up in the air or put them off their aim.

Captain Harry Porter

As you can appreciate, the sky is terribly clear. As a matter of fact, you can see stars in daylight. This particular raid that came over, about 20,000, 22,000 [feet], I think there were probably about seven or eight bombers escorted by maybe ten Zeroes. I can still picture those Zeroes weaving back and forward over the top of the bombers . . . the Zeroes were spotted before the bombers, and the guns took on the Zeroes, which was a bad thing – I mean our job was to try to divert the bombers away from targets . . . but . . . the guns were firing on the Zeroes when they should have been on the bombers. When we realised what was happening, of course, we had to switch targets from the Zeroes onto the bombers, but I can still picture the bright sunlight glinting on these things as they drifted across the top of us.

If you went into a gunsite you usually threw two or three strands of barbed-wire right round the site. The barbed-wire was put far enough away . . . [so] that they couldn't throw a hand grenade into a slit-trench from outside the barbed-wire.

Sergeant Cunningham Fowler

I well remember when they got into our camp – I was at regimental headquarters, and they burned quite a few of our vehicles before we really knew they had arrived. They slipped round the back of the regiments in front of us and came in. Unfortunately, our sentries had missed them getting in among us and that was very frightening. It was after that, I think, that our boys were inclined to throw hand grenades at any noise in the jungle. I didn't blame them either.

Captain Robin Kinahan, *Adjutant, 8th (Belfast)*
Heavy Anti-Aircraft Regiment

The jungle sounds at night still come back in my memory. It was never silent. There was always something going on, some strange animals making noises and the cracking of the bamboo, and you wouldn't know whether it was the Japanese coming in or not, so everybody was absolutely on their toes at night, as well as during the day, because it was a wonderful place to infiltrate . . . without being seen.

Captain Harry Porter

The Burma campaign was fought without conventional front lines. Japanese soldiers could attack the front and rear of a position at the same time, a tactic they used to great effect all over Burma, thereby forcing the Allies to set up strong defensive positions, or 'boxes'. This was not the first time that the defensive box had been used as a military technique; similar tactics had been adopted in the Desert Campaign. The enemy in Burma was an altogether different proposition from the German and Italian soldiers in North Africa, however:

Of course, the Japanese was a completely different animal to what we had met in France: the Germans. They never gave in. I saw one prisoner of war in three and a half years out there. They committed *hari-kari* because they believed, in their religion, that their souls went into an unborn child who would then become a soldier for the emperor.

Captain Harry Porter

I think that the European found it a little difficult to appreciate the

Airfield defence. A 3.7-inch heavy anti-aircraft gun in action on an airstrip in Burma. This was the weapon which equipped 8th (Belfast) Heavy Anti-Aircraft Regiment.

utter dedication, the complete sacrifice of self to the cause, that the Japanese believed in. Their emperor, of course, was divine and the greatest honour that one could give to the Japanese soldier, to award him, was to die for his god, for his emperor. And he must never, in any circumstance, be taken prisoner.

Major Desmond Whyte,
Senior Medical Officer, 111 (Chindit) Brigade

I remember, after I got wounded, they were taking me down to hospital in a jeep and they had things on the jeep for putting stretchers on. They put the Jap on the stretcher outside and I was inside the jeep. We drove down, stopped near the hospital and we got out and we pulled the blanket down off the Jap. He had pulled it over his head . . . and when they lifted him out, he was dead. He must have committed *hari-kari*.

We took a place too . . . from the Japs and we weren't right settled in until we saw a Japanese coming along with a mule and some stuff on the mule. We were sent out to intercept him, four of us. And we got out, he spotted us, grenade to his stomach and he held his arm round the mule and blew the two of them up.

Private Tommy Tracey, 2nd King's Own Scottish Borderers

. . . we moved into a new gunsite on the edge of the jungle and there was a field regiment . . . about half a mile away. About 2.00 in the morning there was a most tremendous uproar, shots going off and yelling and shouting. And we went down to see what was going on. Japanese had come up in two trucks . . . to the sentry of this gunsite where the men were sleeping and had said that they were reinforcements, in perfect English. The sentry let them through and, of course, they were Japanese infantry. There were many casualties there and three guns were blown up. So that was the reason why we had to be on our toes night and day.

Captain Harry Porter

As the Burma campaign continued, the Belfast men were called upon more frequently to perform as field gunners, earning themselves the nickname 'Twelve-Mile Snipers' because their shooting was so accurate. They could not always see their targets, so they enlisted the help of spotter planes. Some of the pilots had an unconventional approach:

> The spotter plane . . . was in a landing-strip that was surrounded entirely along with the four guns and also the command post, the predictors and everything else. [The pilot] was a big Scottish bloke with a black moustache . . . and in this Auster plane, the spotter plane – a very slow plane – he had a radio, a revolver and a bottle of Scotch. His job was to take off from this strip, fly over the Mayu ridge, identify targets and then radio back to our command post whatever height or distance was required. And he told us that on one occasion about eighty-odd Japs were killed, lining up at their cookhouse with their bowls of rice. We didn't see this, of course . . . on another occasion he actually pinpointed a barge coming up a river and we got direct hits on it.
>
> *Gunner Tom Reynolds, Regimental Headquarters,*
> *8th (Belfast) Heavy Anti-Aircraft Regiment*

Before we got spotter planes, which was very near the end of the campaign, we were responsible for our own spotting during the day. So officers, including myself, went out in an observation post [OP] and our job was to radio back to the guns about the fall of shot. The trouble was that the OPs were normally on the top of one of these ridges, and the trajectories of the shells were extremely low, so you could look back over your shoulder when you gave the order to fire to see the four guns fire, and then, about two or three seconds later, hear this thing like an express train actually going over your own head, and then you would correct the shot.

The other thing we used to do . . . [was] harassing fire. We'd range the guns on during the day on some other target so . . . they would be accurate at night and then fire salvoes, all guns going off together. I actually wear the watch on occasions that I used to count down the guns: 'Five . . . four . . . three . . . two . . . one . . . FIRE', and they all used to go off together – a great surprise for the enemy.

Captain Harry Porter

The Belfast Regiment's most historic action was at the Battle of the Boxes in the Arakan in February 1944, when an Allied advance was met with a strong counter-attack from General Hanaya's Japanese soldiers. British and Indian troops were cut off, and there was very fierce fighting, especially at Ngakyedauk Pass, where some of the regiment's guns were used to try to force the enemy out of tunnels in the hills around the pass:

> The Battle of the Boxes, really it's famous because it was the first time when the Japanese got round behind you that you didn't immediately get orders to retreat, as had happened for a year or so. The Japanese technique was to go through the jungle past you, come up behind you [and] cut off your supplies. [One British division] had been over the mountain, through the tunnel . . . they hoped to march down that river valley while we went down the coastal river valley. Well then, of course, when the Japanese came round behind them this box battle started.
>
> *Captain Robin Kinahan*

> I was a troop commander at the time with the guns, trying to get the Japanese out of the tunnels. The trouble was that our guns had a very low trajectory, the shell went very level, not like a mortar, which went up in the air and fell down. The tunnels were surrounded by hills and mountains about up to 1,000 feet high, and you could not fire directly into them, so that was one of the problems.
>
> *Captain Harry Porter*

> They were dug in and had been for quite some time . . . but they were very, very difficult to get out of these tunnels, because they used to run their guns out to the very mouth of the tunnel, fire and then retreat back in. Well, they tried all sorts, heavy artillery, twenty-five pounders, three-point-sevens, everything, and couldn't move them. And then, of course, there were these Vultee Vengeance, the Indian Air Force, Sikh pilots, who used to come over every day at 4.00 pm on the dot. They would peel off and dive-bomb the entrance to the tunnel, and then . . . the artillery would follow. But eventually they had to use flame-throwers.
>
> *Gunner Tom Reynolds*

> I went through the tunnels when I heard they'd been opened, and it was very messy. I can remember the smell of the dead, both Japanese

and our own people, as we got out on the other side. It really was a very bloody battle.

Captain Robin Kinahan

As the Allied army forced the enemy back in the Arakan, a similar strategy was being used further north. In the Battles of Kohima and Imphal, General Slim's Fourteenth Army held the Indian border against the forces of the Japanese commander, General Mutaguchi, who had launched Operation U-GO, the March on Delhi.

During these battles attempts were made to cut off the Japanese supply routes in a number of ways, including the use of long-range infantry penetration into the Burmese jungle. One of the elite forces sent in were the Chindits. Their job was to harass the Japanese; however, the situation at Kohima and Imphal was so dangerous that one Chindit brigade was ordered to create its own box behind the Japanese lines in order to cut off supplies to Mutaguchi's men. This box, or strong point, was code-named 'Blackpool':

Within forty-eight hours, at night, the enemy attacked from the north east, and there was very unpleasant fighting. We had our barbed-wire emplacements down by then and the enemy retired before dawn, having sustained very heavy casualties. The enemy came back in greater numbers the following night and broke through in several places. That was repulsed, and when the sun came up . . . the unpleasantness . . . I don't know if one should enlarge on this, but flesh doesn't last very long in the heat and, by now, the early rain. We were coming into May and the monsoon was breaking. That in itself was exceedingly unpleasant.

Our condition was far from ideal . . . we were worn down physically, we were all full of malaria, we were under suppressive treatment with a view to keeping the malaria in check . . . jungle sores, you'd get a small scratch, it would begin to ulcerate; leachbites, which were ever present, would go septic; the jaundice, infective jaundice, began to make itself felt; and there were the usual bowel complaints which were very unpleasant and very wearing.

Lack of sleep was probably the worst [problem], that and insufficient food. We were living on a thing called K Ration and we were burning up to 6,000 calories a day, heavy marching with a seventy-pound load, and, of course, the K Ration was not designed for this sort of warfare.

'The Twelfth', a long way from home. The Belfast Regiment moved to Ranchi, East Bengal, in 1944 to replace its guns and took the opportunity to celebrate the Twelfth. The pipe-band was the regiment's own and the banners were made from ammunition covers. Both Catholic and Protestant soldiers took part in the celebrations.

It was a temporary emergency ration, and we were living off our own fat, on the downgrade.

By the time we got to 'Blackpool' our physical condition was far from ideal, but morale was high. We believed we were the elite, that's what kept us going. But how sad to watch close colleagues, friends . . . just the flame of life gradually flickering, and you'd awaken after three or four hours when the alert was sounded and your friend was dead beside you. The flame of life had gone. That was sad.

Major Desmond Whyte

While the Japanese attacked Blackpool, Desmond Whyte and his fellow doctors continued to treat the wounded and maimed in spite of the heavy shelling, which threatened the lives of wounded and medical officers alike. Supplies of medicine and food were parachuted in, but at times even these supply lines were cut off.

One of the ever-present difficulties was the need to evacuate the badly wounded; thanks to the ingenuity of the American air force it was possible to evacuate some of the wounded out of Blackpool:

We had gliders, and once the glider landed . . . in the ordinary course of events it was written off. But our American friends had worked out a plan some time before the invasion into Burma whereby it was possible to attach a loop to the front of the glider . . . that loop was hung on two poles that were fifteen-feet high, each with a little bulb at the top with a battery that they would light at night; by day they didn't need them. You now had two poles sticking up with a light at the top of either, and the loop was hung across the top of that – the bottom part, of course, being attached to the glider. And the specially equipped Dakota had a great hook sticking out from the back with a very strong spring drum. And, I actually watched this, we'd load our wounded in, the plane would come down, make two or three false runs and then, to your great relief, the glider would be suddenly hooked, rather like a salmon, in a way, and it would go off. We never saw them again, of course. We had no idea whether they ever made it, we had other things to think about.

Major Desmond Whyte

On 25 May 1944, 111 Chindit Brigade was withdrawn from Blackpool, just before the Battle of Kohima ended. Imphal was relieved on 22 June and General Slim's army was able to turn its attention to the recapture of Burma. However, the Japanese soldier was as tough an opponent when retreating as when he was advancing, and every strong point had to be fought for fiercely:

> . . . it was a steady battle all the way . . . because up in these hills it took you all night to get up to the top, and when you got to the top they were waiting for you. There was always a battle there. Pushed on again . . . the next night, same thing again, same thing again, until eventually we got . . . them out.
>
> Then we had to cross the Irrawaddy and then we started pushing down through Burma. Brigades were spread all over Burma, but we were on the flanks . . . pushed right down, and every village you came to they were waiting for you, and that was another battle. The huts were built up on stilts, I'm surmising, to let the monsoon water go underneath, and they were underneath that and scattered all over the place. You had to attack them.
>
> When you moved them out of that the chase started again and it was going on like that for days and days. When they were moving out of a village they always left a *hari-kari* squad behind them – maybe, say, five or six men. They could hold you up long enough until you killed them all and let the main body get away.
>
> We sent out a patrol to see how they were getting up their supplies. They never came back and we had to go out and look for them. We got them but the only one recognisable was big Jock McDonald, because he had red hair and it was right [along] the top of his chest, way up to his neck. That's how we recognised Jock. Most of our men [were] always prepared to do themselves in, they always kept one up the spout to use on yourself before you would let them get you.
>
> *Private Tommy Tracey*

On 13 February 1945 Fourteenth Army crossed the Irrawaddy River south of Mandalay and by 13 March they had cut the Japanese escape route. Mandalay was relieved a week later, and by May Pegu and Prome had fallen. Allied forces were now advancing south to Rangoon. The Japanese, however, were still inflicting casualties on their opponents:

> We'd cleared a village of them, pushed them on through the jungle and

they had got behind trees. The jungle was pretty thick, we had blades to cut our way through, and I was a wee bit in front and I spotted a Jap. I moved behind a tree and went to move again and he got me, got me through the shoulder. Then the boys coming up on the flank, they got him. I had to wait then for a while and they got a jeep up, they were able to use jeeps there, took me down then to a forward hospital, just a small place that had moved up behind the fighting . . . they treated it there a wee bit and we were eventually flown out.

Private Tommy Tracey

On 6 August and 9 August, as General Slim's troops prepared for the assault on Rangoon and the final battle with the Japanese in Burma, atomic bombs were dropped on Hiroshima and Nagasaki, leading to the Japanese surrender. It took until 28 August for the Rangoon garrison to surrender, and the final Japanese surrender in Burma took place on 13 September 1945.

I was just out of the hospital and I hadn't reached the battalion, when somebody came in and said the war was over. We just couldn't believe it, couldn't believe it. I was getting set to go back . . . up to Burma again, to the battalion, but instead of that I went up to Peshawar, up to the frontier. There [were] so many of the boys I'd come out with [that] had all gone, and I was still there. But I never thought I would have survived and I'm sure most of the fellas in Burma didn't think they were going to survive either.

. . . when I was coming home altogether we used to sleep in hammocks on the boat. I couldn't sleep this night and I got up. I was sitting on deck coming through the Indian Ocean, big moon, water lapping on the sides, and the first thing I heard was one of the crew putting on a record, he must have had a gramophone: 'Home, Sweet Home', Deanna Durban.

Private Tommy Tracey

The Quiet Hero

While 111 Chindit Brigade was besieged in the Blackpool Block, one man's heroism was an inspiration to everyone, so much so that the brigade commander, John Masters, later a famous novelist, and the commanders of each of the infantry battalions jointly wrote a citation recommending the award of the Victoria Cross to **Major Desmond Whyte**, their senior medical officer. In his book *The Road Past Mandalay*, Masters described Desmond Whyte as 'the man who, above all others, has kept the brigade going . . . but Desmond has not dashed out and rescued one wounded man under fire, he has only saved two hundred over a hundred days, calm and efficient and cheerful while shells blast the bodies to pieces under his hands.'

Masters was understandably annoyed when Desmond Whyte was awarded the Distinguished Service Order (DSO) rather than the VC: 'This is not good enough', he wrote. Desmond Whyte has never begrudged the fact that he did not receive the VC. He was, in his view, only doing his job. How well he did that job can be seen from the *London Gazette* entry for his DSO.

> Major Whyte . . . was in command of 'Blackpool' Medical Dressing Station from the 7th to the 25th of May 1944.
> . . . the fortress was under continual attack by enemy infantry, mortars, machine-guns, artillery and aircraft. The garrison suffered numerous casualties, all of which passed through the Medical Dressing Station. The Medical Dressing Station was hit several times by shell fire and patients [were] killed. Continuous rain made conditions for patients and doctors bad. There was a chronic and continual shortage of all medical stores. Evacuation of a proportion of patients was carried out from an airstrip; on at least two occasions under enemy fire, Major Whyte supervised the evacuation.
> Throughout this period Major Whyte showed complete disregard of his personal safety and gave a superb and sustained

example of cheerfulness and courage. He treated patients in his Medical Dressing Station and went out on shell and machine-gun swept slopes to collect and treat them.

On the 25th of May 1944, when 'Blackpool' was evacuated, he organised the evacuation of wounded, including stretcher cases. During the evacuation twelve patients and stretcher bearers were killed in the immediate vicinity of Major Whyte, who continued his work as if nothing was happening.

From the 25th to the 29th May 1944, Major Whyte organised the carriage, movement and treatment of 180 wounded men, mostly without equipment, blankets or cover of any kind, with inadequate medical equipment, over 18 miles of muddy mountain track in continuous pouring rain, without food.

This Officer's continuous courage and cheerfulness was an inspiration to the wounded, many of whom would have succumbed but for him and the other Brigade Medical Officers.

Hero of the Blackpool block and the Chindit Brigade's Senior Medical Officer, Desmond Whyte. At the time this photograph was taken, Lieutenant Colonel Whyte was the chief medical officer of the Indian Airborne Division, whose insignia can be seen on his sleeve. The oak-leaf emblem of a Mention-in-Dispatches figures on the medal ribbon on the left.

7
War at Sea

It was pretty scary, and I know I was scared a lot of times.

BEFORE the Second World War started, German surface ships were waiting in the sea lanes to Europe to cut off the lifeline to Britain and France. One of the earliest German raiders was the pocket battleship *Admiral Graf Spee*. *Graf Spee* was finally hunted down in South America, where its captain scuttled his ship at the mouth of the River Plate rather than face the ships waiting outside. This action highlighted the vulnerability of the German surface fleet. It also demonstrated that for the Royal Navy there was never a period of Phoney War at sea as there was on land in Europe.

With the vulnerability of their surface units exposed, the Germans were reluctant to use them to any great extent and began to concentrate on their submarine or U-boat fleet. These became the greatest threat to Allied shipping, and convoys had to be formed to protect merchant ships crossing the Atlantic. Many of the ships which operated as escorts to convoys from America to Britain were based in Belfast and Londonderry, and the latter became the most vital escort base in the United Kingdom.

The Battle of the Atlantic was the most important campaign of the war – Britain's survival depended on supplies coming in by sea. It was only to be expected, then, that the major part of the Royal Navy's war was spent protecting convoys in the Atlantic; nevertheless, its ships were also needed in every corner of the globe. One area where the navy was very heavily engaged was in the Mediterranean; there its role was to protect Britain's Middle Eastern oil supplies. Naval operations in the region were conducted from three main ports: Gibraltar, Malta and Alexandria. After Italy declared war in June 1940, Allied shipping in the Mediterranean was in danger from the powerful Italian fleet, which was much bigger than the German surface fleet.

Alex. The harbour of Alexandria, home to the Mediterranean Fleet, from the air; in the forefront flies a Fairey Swordfish of the Fleet Air Arm.

At about that time seventeen-year-old **Billy Jarvis** went to Belfast to join the Royal Navy:

> I was seventeen at the time and I had to wait until I was seventeen and a half. They wouldn't accept me in the army, so I applied to get into the navy and there I was. We did ten weeks' training down in Devonport and then we were sent up to Rosyth, and everyone on that ship was given leave except me. The reason they didn't give me any leave was because I was Irish, they thought I wouldn't come back again. If I had known what I was going into I wouldn't have come back.
>
> But anyway, we were then sent up to Scapa Flow and joined this cruiser, the *York*, and she set off on route to the Middle East. We had all been given injections against typhus and typhoid and . . . our arms had swollen up terribly and . . . were very painful and we were all seasick. These hardened sailors on board used to come down and we'd be lying there really sick, anybody that's ever been seasick will know what I mean. They had big plates of pork and bacon and it made us worse. Every so often they would announce over the ship's radio, 'We are now in such and such a position.' Coming out of Scapa Flow into the Atlantic it was really rough, and I heard the voice saying, 'We are now 300-odd miles off the north-west coast of Ireland', and I thought, 'God, if I could swim, I would swim home tonight.' But after a few days we got used to it.
>
> Our first port of call was in Freetown. I'd been reading up about the jungle and Tarzan and all. My God, what a let down! It was stinking, the smell of it was awful. We were ferried ashore in motorboats to the local . . . pub, if you could call it that, and this big man was standing, dressed in naval whites . . . on the landing-stage, and I heard him saying, 'Now, you go that way, and hi, hi, you, get you that way there', and I thought, 'an Irish voice' . . . I was the only Irishman on this big cruiser. I went up to him and I said, 'Excuse me, are you Irish?' 'Naw,' he said, 'I'm not, I'm from Ballymena.' That finished me off altogether.

After travelling around the entire African coastline HMS *York* sailed northwards through the Suez Canal, destined for the Mediterranean Fleet's main anchorage, Alexandria:

We were in a cruiser squadron which operated out of Alexandria and as far as Malta with convoys, and, in between times, the fleet would make sweeps up through the Aegean and the Dodecanese, which were hotbeds of German and Italian airfields. The Italians were inclined to keep high up, they were terrific at high-level bombing, but the German pilots . . . very brave men, they were coming in with torpedo-bombers, dive-bombers, high-level bombers. They threw everything at us, especially if we were going with a convoy.

It was a hell of a sight, seeing the whole fleet, the *Illustrious*, the big aircraft-carrier, and all the ships all steaming along and all turning, doing a zig-zag to avoid torpedoes. Then suddenly you'd see the line of flags going up on the admiral-in-charge's ship, and you knew then: Action Stations! You could sit and watch them coming down and trying to bomb the *Illustrious* . . . at that particular time the cards were stacked very heavily against the forces in the Middle East, and we were kept pretty much on the go all the time.

The constant threat of the Italian fleet and, from early 1941, the German air force – the Luftwaffe – kept the Mediterranean Fleet on the alert during convoy duties and on its frequent patrols. During one such patrol Billy Jarvis's ship encountered two Italian cruisers:

Those Italian ships, when we come on them, they didn't put [up] any fight at all. Naturally enough, when they were spotted our ships opened up on them . . . and as soon as the battle started they ran up a white flag, but by that time we had started to shell the [first] ship. There was another one . . . but they were all jumping over the side and we were laying off and shelling and then this white flag went up and stopped and the ship blew up. [Our] captain . . . ordered scrambling nets out and then the word came through a couple of minutes later: 'No, reverse that order, German planes in the vicinity.' And we had to steam away and leave those people. You couldn't afford to stop, you'd be a sitting target for any aircraft that [were] coming over. So, you just went on.

It was tough, but that was it. You either stayed and got sunk yourself or badly damaged, or else got out of the way. I honestly don't know what happened to those men, but we didn't stop to pick them up. You

HMS *York* rests on the bottom of Suda Bay in Crete. After being damaged by the Italian navy, the cruiser was also bombed and set on fire. Scorch marks can be seen in the photograph.

couldn't do it. I've seen plenty of bodies floating in the water. We came along one time and this corpse was floating face down. It was a German pilot, and his whole underside was covered in barnacles but the back of him, his uniform and all, you would have thought he was just floating in the water until we turned him over. It wasn't a very nice sight . . . when I saw my first couple of dead bodies it was just after Dunkirk and we were down on the south coast of England at Chatham. We were sent out to help . . . clear ships . . . and there were bodies on boats that were brought in. I was really . . . well, I was sick, looking at them, but then, when you got a few tots of rum in you, you didn't care. It was rough.

Billy Jarvis's ship survived that encounter with the Italian navy, but on their next meeting, on the north-west coast of Crete, *York* was not so lucky. Recalls Jarvis:

We put into Suda Bay and that night there was a tanker, called the *Pericles*, lying in the same anchorage, and a couple of other boats and ourselves, and the captain announced over the loudspeaker system, 'We've just had word that the Italian fleet has left its anchorage and we hope to start tomorrow morning very early and go out and engage them.'

We were all exhausted. Quite a few of us were in quarters up in the fore part of the ship, and about 2.00 in the morning there was this unearthly explosion. The Italians had devised a weapon . . . they packed the bows of a motorboat with explosives and all around the outside of it they had detonators, and they just aimed the nose of the motorboat at the target, pulled a lever and they floated off on their seat, but the steering was locked and this is what hit us.

We didn't know what it was. We thought it was aircraft and we tried to get out of the fore part of the boat and we couldn't because somebody had closed the watertight door. I could feel the ship sinking, but fortunately for us it wasn't too deep there and she just settled on the bottom. But the whole armour-plating of the deck was like a ripple effect. We must have been in there for about half an hour trying to get out of that place but we couldn't. The tanker that I told you about, they hit that too, and it just went up in flames. The cruiser I was on was finished, that was her.

York's crew were then given a variety of jobs on Crete, which was being heavily attacked by the Luftwaffe in preparation for an invasion of the island. *York*'s guns were used to bolster the anti-aircraft defences of Crete, and Billy Jarvis ended up boiling water for anti-aircraft gunners, which led to a timely meeting:

> I was the only Irishman on board the boat and was very homesick. There was no mail getting through and the Germans were bombing the island all the time. Sitting outside this cavalry barracks one day this friend of mine and I, we were responsible for keeping a big boiler going with hot water for soldiers to come down from surrounding gun positions to have a bath. I was sitting outside feeling very sorry for myself when I heard this broad Derry voice saying, 'What about a cuppa tay?' . . . when I heard the voice it was like God talking to me, I was so glad to hear it and I called out, 'Is there anybody there from Derry?' 'Aye, who's that?' And it was a gentleman from the Bogside. I didn't care what he was, I was so delighted to hear that Derry voice.

Crete was eventually invaded by the Germans, who forced the Allied troops down into the south of the island where most were safely evacuated to Alexandria. On the retreat many had been helped by the islanders:

> The Cretans were very brave, too. They did everything they could. We had to walk about . . . twenty miles, over the mountains from Suda Bay to get away and they helped us all the way, they really did. And I think they suffered for it afterwards.

After his return to Alexandria Billy Jarvis was posted to a small gunboat, HMS *Cricket*. Although the gunboat's duties were as dangerous as those of the *York*, life on board *Cricket* was more cramped but a lot less impersonal than it had been on the cruiser:

> On the big cruiser, well there [were] over 400 men on it, and your immediate friends were in the mess deck that you were in . . . of course, you went and had a drink with these [other] fellas if you met them outside, but it was generally the people in the mess that you were in that you palled about with, you went ashore with and had a drink with.

The smaller ship was more like a family. It was so small you had to live like a family. Even getting into a bunk you had to be lifted up and put in sideways. You couldn't turn in it once you got in, it was so small. The facilities on it were very basic. It was just an old barge of a thing, but I suppose it did the job. Everytime we fired the six-inch gun the deck split, that's how old it was. But we seemed to be nearer the hard core, if you could call it that, of the war with taking these men up and getting in close [to] shore, and all this.

On the cruiser we were inclined to lay offshore a good bit and shell from, maybe, two or three miles out. It was a different sort of set-up altogether. On the big ship every man did his job, and there was no time for any socialising, but on the small ship we were so dilapidated that we didn't do the same amount of operations that the big ship would do. Maybe we'd go up about once every fortnight, up to Tobruk, and land soldiers or supplies or go up and do a bit of bombarding and then come back. But that was all, and of course she only lasted about six trips. She was a flea in the German ear because they used to use the coast road above Tobruk, and this is what we were shelling . . . to try to prevent them from using them.

Cricket's duties involved shelling the *Via Balbia*, the main supply route for the German forces besieging Tobruk. This kept the gunboat fairly close to land, but there were times when the army asked the navy to assist with raids behind enemy lines; this could involve some of *Cricket*'s crew coming right onto dry land. According to Jarvis:

We were detailed off to take Australian commandos up and to land them behind the German lines. The gunboat couldn't get inshore, the water was too shallow, so we had to row them and then, when they got ashore, the whalers, the boats that had brought them in, had to lay offshore. There were men detailed off to stay ashore to give these fellows covering fire . . . three of us were . . . to do it.

It was pretty nerve-wracking, and while we were walking up and down this beach we heard the gunfire and explosions from inland. We thought this was the boys doing their stuff. Of course, as the time wore on we got more and more, I was going to say nervous, but to tell you the truth it was scared. We got more and more scared and I kept looking out to make sure the boat was waiting on us, and suddenly, out of nowhere, this hand came round my mouth. I nearly collapsed. It was the boys coming back and they thought this was a good joke.

One of them had been shot through the head – the temple – and the bullet went in one side and come out the other. Going back down to Mersa Matruh, he was sitting smoking on the upper deck [with] the two patches of sticking plaster on each side of his head. So, he must have been very lucky.

But I'll tell you, it was pretty scary, somebody coming up behind you and you standing there waiting for something to happen, you didn't know who it was . . . that night I didn't need any castor-oil, let me put it that way.

The Germans had gained a very strong foothold in the Mediterranean and their air force threatened the very existence of Allied shipping in the region, so much so that Malta was virtually cut off. On one trip to Tobruk the gunboat *Cricket* experienced the force and ferocity of a full-scale attack from the air. Against the might of such an attack, it had little to defend itself with other than light anti-aircraft guns and some captured Italian weapons:

We had about a dozen of those all round the ship, and it was only a small gun, slightly larger than a sten-gun. Our captain, he kept his own personal Lewis-gun on the bridge and we had a six-inch gun which was useless for anti-aircraft work. We had an Oerlikon gun, one on the port and one on the starboard side, and I would nearly say that was it. That's what we had to fight off these Stukas . . . at that time, 1940 and 1941, there was very little getting through from the supplies. You just had to make do with what you had.

It wasn't a big convoy. It was just three or four ships and we were supposed to be supporting them. I was cook of the day and I had got the dinner all ready and was taking it up to put it in the galley and we heard the four warning shots from one of the other vessels. This was a signal that there was enemy aircraft about. I looked up and the sky seemed to be filled with Stuka dive-bombers. They started and they attacked us all in turn and that went on . . . from about 11.00 am until about 3.00 in the afternoon.

They were very brave men, there was no doubt about it. They aimed their aircraft at the target and they had a contraption on the wings of these Stukas which created a most awful screaming;

it was like a demented banshee. The noise of it penetrated your brain . . . it's indescribable, but it was awful, the bombs exploding, guns banging and this screaming noise, and then when they reached a certain level they released the bomb and pulled up out of the dive and the bomb went on.

At about 3.00 in the afternoon this fella came down and just before it, I remember seeing one of these planes coming along at water-level, and I don't know if I'm imagining it, or was imagining it, but I could see puffs of smoke coming from his guns and I could see the shells hitting the water in front of where I was standing. I was sure that was our lot. They dropped this bomb and it came down, went through one of our whalers . . . and exploded underneath the ship and it blew us right out of the water.

We came down like a piece of wood that you shove into the water, it goes down under, you push it down, and it bounces back up. It blew the whole bottom out of the gunboat and there were seven men killed. One man in particular was blown over the side, and just before we'd left on that trip he'd got a letter from home to say that his wife had given birth to their first child. The last I saw of him, or any of us saw of him, he was being carried away. We couldn't stop to pick him up.

They blew the whole bottom out of the boat, but because she was so wide that's what saved us. And they still kept coming back and machine-gunning and bombing. I honestly don't know how we ever made it back to Alexandria but we did. That was more or less the end of my war in the Middle East. It was really rough, really rough, not what we thought it would be, like you would read in the *Wizard* or the *Hotspur*. It was dirty, it was terrifying and I wouldn't want to go through it again . . .

The Royal Navy continued to be involved in the Mediterranean for several more years. The landings in Sicily and later in Italy needed the support of the navy, whose heavy ships could use their guns to bombard shore targets in support of the ground forces. At the same time smaller ships protected the amphibious forces against submarines.

Elsewhere its ships fought the German and Japanese navies constantly, until peace returned in August 1945. The Royal Navy had been in action almost from the day that war was declared, and the experiences of Billy Jarvis were typical of those of the many Ulstermen whose war was fought at sea:

Me and all my friends, we seemed to have the idea that it was going to be like something you would see in the movies; there was no blood, no planes coming straight at you and this thing screaming in your ears; there was no bodies floating in the sea and you had to pass by them. It was the direct opposite of everything that we thought it would be. It was just hell on earth, but again it didn't happen all the time . . . when it did happen it was pretty scary, and I know I was scared a lot of times. To me it was a moment of terror and an hour of relief that your name wasn't on the bomb or the bullet that was aimed at you, relief to know that you were going to make it another day. Apart from the action part of it, the friendships that I made and, something that I never could have afforded myself: I've seen parts of the world that I never would have seen – Africa, south, east and west, Greece, Malta, the West Indies, places like that; it was great, but again I was glad to get home.

I always remember when I came home for my first leave after nearly three years and I got on the train in Belfast, and the train was coming along, and I remember as it turned the bay . . . at Rosses Bay, and there was the beautiful Foyle and the green hills and the two churches and their spires. I actually cried when I saw that – it was so beautiful to me after the desert and the sandstorms and the whirlwinds and all the rest of it, and that sight of Derry to me was beautiful . . . . It was a wonderful end to my bit of war. Anyway, I thought so.

Belfast's Sailor Hero

Days before the end of the war in the Far East, Ulster's second Victoria Cross of the war was won by a sailor. **Leading Seaman James Joseph Magennis** from Belfast's Falls Road district earned the VC for his gallantry on 31 July 1945, when he attached limpet mines to the Japanese cruiser *Takao* in the Johore Straits.

Magennis, a diver, had entered the straits in the midget submarine XE3 with **Lieutenant Ian Fraser**. The Belfastman left the sub, squeezing through a narrow gap in the partly opened hatch, to fix the mine to the cruiser. His breathing apparatus was leaking, but in spite of this Magennis scraped barnacles from the bottom of *Takao* to secure the mine. When he returned to the submarine he was exhausted from his labours. As they prepared to withdraw, Lieutenant Fraser found that one of the charges still attached to the submarine could not be released; Magennis volunteered to go out again to remove the charge. It took five minutes' work with a heavy spanner to accomplish this dangerous task, but Magennis succeeded and XE3 was able to escape to safety.

Magennis was the only person from Northern Ireland to win a VC in the Second World War.

Leading Seaman James Joseph Magennis, VC, whose courage led to the destruction of the Japanese cruiser *Takao*, just weeks before the end of the war.

8

War in the Skies

An aircraft just in front of us got a direct hit and blew up in mid-air.

THE ROYAL AIR FORCE was involved in active operations from the beginning of the Second World War. Fighter Command aircraft mounted constant patrols to guard against the possibility of German aircraft bombing Britain. Bomber Command, however, was forbidden to drop bombs on Germany by Chamberlain's government and was restricted to dropping propaganda leaflets on German cities to try to turn German public opinion against the war. Active operations for the bombers included dropping sea-mines off the German coastline and attacking German shipping.

For Coastal Command's crews the first day of war was the beginning of a campaign against German submarines destined to last until peace returned in 1945. Among the Coastal Command units involved from the outbreak of war was 502 (Ulster) Squadron, which was based at Aldergrove and, later, at Limavady on the shores of Lough Foyle. Its job was to patrol the north-west sea approaches in order to protect convoys:

> When the squadron changed over to Whitleys, longer range, we used to do nine, ten-hour patrols into the Atlantic. At times you took off in the dark in the winter, 5.00, 6.00 in the evening, and didn't get back until maybe 5.00 or 6.00 the next morning. So you were flying in the dark all the time, although you had a second pilot with you, and a lot of that flying was done on instruments. It got a bit monotonous at times.
>
> In fact, I was inclined, sometimes, to almost doze off. Flying on instruments all the time . . . mesmerised you . . . and if you were very tired you could almost go to sleep. We had automatic pilots which weren't . . . very good at all on the Whitleys. You could be flying along

and suddenly the thing went out of gear and the nose went down; you had to pull yourself together and get the stick back quickly before you went into the sea.

Squadron-Leader Hunter McGiffin, 502 (Ulster) Squadron

After the BEF's evacuation from France in June 1940, Fighter Command fought the battle against the German air force in the skies over southern England. That autumn the Luftwaffe changed its tactics to night bombing, which lasted until May 1941. Towards the end of that night *blitz*, the most serious casualties suffered by any city outside London were inflicted on Belfast on the night of 14 and the early morning of 15 April.

Bomber Command was, by then, attacking German cities, while Fighter Command was able to change from protecting Britain's skies to attacking German forces in occupied France. One of their roles was low-level photographic reconnaissance:

You had to photograph, preferably, somewhere between 500 and 1,000 feet. Sometimes you had to go slightly higher than that. We did that in pairs. One pilot stayed above, just circling round so that you couldn't be bounced. You would get maximum speed, from a dive probably [from] about 5,000 or 6,000 feet. You would dive down over the port and do a half turn round it . . . and operate your camera, which was on the stick. It was quite easy to operate, [the camera] was on the side of the Spitfire; you just tilted the Spitfire so you were flying round naturally and you took your photographs.

. . . they did an awful lot of firing of flak; you got everything thrown at you, including the coastal batteries, and we lost a few pilots that way. You normally got . . . some minor type of a hit, and sometimes you escaped, but it was difficult to fly through all the flak without being hit sometimes.

Flight-Lieutenant Bill Pauley, 501 Fighter Squadron

The Royal Navy had its own aircraft in the Fleet Air Arm, which not only helped protect Allied shipping but also worked with the RAF, supporting ground forces during landing operations:

The first trip I very nearly had a head-on collision with an Me109. He was more shaken probably than I was, but luckily we both picked the right way and passed a few feet apart. We were just in the process of dropping our 'jet' tanks, which meant we had to throttle back and have the engine at coarse pitch so that we were going at minimum speed. It was ten-tenths cloud at about 2,000 feet and this Messerschmitt Me109 came diving out of the cloud at 300 or 400 miles an hour, absolutely going straight for me. He turned to port and I turned to port, too, so that we went belly-to-belly past each other; it must have been only a matter of feet. And then we turned . . . and chased after him. He disappeared in the distance towards Paris.

Lieutenant George Boyd, 885 Naval Air Squadron

While the bomber and fighter crews were fighting the war over Europe, Coastal Command's airmen continued their difficult and often boring patrols in the Battle of the Atlantic. Their boredom could be broken by attacks on U-boats or the presence of Luftwaffe aircraft:

One morning I was approaching a convoy well out in the Atlantic when I saw a lot of smoke coming up from one of the merchant vessels in the centre of the convoy. It was on fire and just as I got near the convoy an aircraft came in the other direction, practically head-on to me. It was a Focke-Wulf Condor that had just bombed this vessel. These Condors flew from the north of France, right round the west of Ireland and round the north of Scotland to Norway. If they met a convoy they then reported it by radio, and the U-boats were homed onto it . . . in this instance this plane passed so close I could see the pilot in it, but by the time I turned round – my aircraft was rather a slow one and he was rather fast – I couldn't get near him. I think we loosed off a few rounds from the front gun but that was no use at all.

Squadron-Leader Hunter McGiffin

The danger from the Condors made gun-crews on Allied ships over-eager to open fire on any aircraft that came within threatening distance of the convoys:

If you got too near a convoy, the navy – either they weren't too good at aircraft recognition or else they just played on the safe side – but they would shoot off at you. In fact, I was out in a destroyer during the war in the Atlantic; they used to come and fly with us, the escort commanders,

Hunter McGiffin commanded 502 (Ulster) Squadron, Royal Auxiliary Air Force, after the war. In this photograph he can be seen, in black overalls, in front of one of the squadron's Mosquitos.

and we used to go on their ships occasionally for experience. One day one of our aircraft got rather close to this ship and the commander said to me – I was on the bridge – 'I should open fire on that aircraft.' I said, 'Sir, what about your aircraft recognition?' 'Well,' he said, 'he's within 1,500 yards and he shouldn't be there. I'm entitled to open fire on him.'

Squadron-Leader Hunter McGiffin

U-boats were the greatest threat, but there were times when German surface ships presented considerable danger. One such vessel was the biggest battleship of its time, the *Bismarck*. It interrupted a short night's sleep for Hunter McGiffin in May 1941:

I was living out with my wife at that time in rooms in Limavady and I remember well getting to bed at 2.05 am and at 2.07 my telephone beside the bed rang and they said, 'Down to the operations room at once, urgent!' I leapt out of bed and [went] down to the ops room at the airfield. They said, 'The *Bismarck* is coming in towards Brittany. You've got to fly down to St Eval', which was in Cornwall.

So we all got into our aircraft and everybody was in good form . . . and we all took off and flew down to Cornwall. Luckily, when we got there and went in, the first thing they said was, 'She's been rounded up by the navy and is just about sunk, so you don't have to go out', which was a rather good job because I think if we had, we'd have been in trouble with her anti-aircraft guns. So we turned round, had breakfast at St Eval, flew back and were in Limavady again by lunch-time. That's how we sank the *Bismarck*.

Squadron-Leader Hunter McGiffin

As the Allies prepared for the invasion of Europe in 1944 fighter squadrons were given the job of protecting bombers that were attacking German installations and supply routes in France and the Low Countries. Those fighters flying closest to the bombers were themselves protected against the threat of German fighter aircraft:

You weren't allowed to chase them. You could . . . engage them if they stayed or intercept them if they were going for the bombers, but you weren't allowed to go in a long pursuit. Mostly they were coming down from above, very high and very fast and, really, chasing after them would have been a waste of time, especially the 190s.

The only thing that we had was the Tempest, and that was later, which would have caught them in a dive. The Tempest had a very high-speed dive but the 190 would out-dive a Spitfire. A Spitfire had manoeuvrability and so on, but it couldn't dive the way a Focke-Wulf 190 could. So really, it would have been a waste of time chasing after them anyway, but if they stayed to engage the bombers then you had to stay with them.

Always, over the continent, there were ranging squadrons, sometimes wings, flying almost out of sight, over 30,000 [feet], so that there was always a presence somewhere. So if there was a concentration of enemy aircraft coming in they would have immediately been deployed down to help because, obviously, Group at home were able to pinpoint the concentrations.

If it was only two or three enemy aircraft doing a sneak attack you didn't worry, but . . . if for some reason the Germans had gathered up a wing of their aircraft and had sent them out determinedly after some bombers coming in over the coast, they'd have squadrons coming from all over the country and more would have been scrambled from 11 Group. So there would have been a hornets' nest in about ten minutes.

Flight-Lieutenant Bill Pauley

Such raids were carried out by light and medium bombers, but the heavy bombers were, at the same time, flying deep into the European mainland to bomb strategic targets in Germany itself. By this stage Hunter McGiffin had become an advanced flying instructor in England; during a visit to a bomber base in Yorkshire, he and three other instructors talked themselves onto a bombing raid on the Ruhr:

[That] morning we went in for briefing and when they dropped the cover off the map we found it was Essen, much to everybody's horror, because that was a most uncomfortable place to go to, with its anti-aircraft defences . . . we took off at about dusk and went out over the Yorkshire coast with hundreds of four-engined bombers all round us . . . to a rendezvous point on the North Sea, and then turned south, right down to Essen.

We dropped our bombs over Essen, which was very well lit up with fires, searchlights, anti-aircraft fire coming up and so on. In fact, an aircraft just in front of us got a direct hit and blew up in mid-air. I never really worried; you always think the other chap will get hit but not you. I think this applied quite a lot. I always felt quite safe in an aircraft, which was all wrong, I suppose, but I never thought we were going to be hit.

But that was the only trip I did on bombers. It was interesting, I was always glad I'd done it, but that night, out of the twelve aircraft we sent out we lost three. A squadron-leader from Canada, Squadron-Leader Boucher, didn't come back. When we got back to Central Flying School we were on the mat, told we shouldn't have gone on this trip, told they couldn't afford to lose experienced instructors.

Squadron-Leader Hunter McGiffin

In the weeks before the invasion of France most of the Allied air power concentrated on attacking German fortifications and communications. The invasion took place on 6 June 1944; two days later Fleet Air Arm pilots were ordered to stop attacking ground targets:

We lost several aircraft through ground-strafing, which we weren't supposed to do. In fact, after D plus two we were forbidden to ground-strafe, because that was when you were vulnerable, when you were low. We did a bit of strafing on D-Day. You couldn't resist it. Once you'd done your shoot and were going back home, if you had enough fuel and you saw anything moving you would've had a go at it until that was stopped.

The main job was spotting for the ships, but after some days all those targets were sorted out and we did a couple of fighter sweeps with the RAF. We did one down the Cherbourg peninsula but, unfortunately, before we got along there the RAF Typhoons had been before us, and [all] the roads the length of the Cherbourg peninsula were littered with German vehicles, smouldering and burning.

There was a factory at Ouistreham and the ship that I was spotting with was the gunboat or monitor, *Erebus*. They called the shots, they really didn't need me to spot. After giving the map reference and saying there was a factory with thirteen bays and they were aiming for the third bay from the left, they would say, 'splash', and, sure enough, they hit the third bay from the left. I said, 'Right, we're moving up to the next row, the sixth bay from the left', and the shot would hit that.

I've never seen anything like the accuracy of the shooting. It was such a difference from the Americans'. The RT code – we would always speak using these code-phrases – for a bad shot was 'lousy', and you used to put a lot of feeling into that word 'lousy' when you were reporting back to the American ships.

Lieutenant George Boyd

You couldn't relax at any time. If you did relax you got a bad fright or maybe you paid for it. We had quite a few of our pilots shot down, some just innocently going over one of the French coasts and guns getting them . . . things could be very quiet and you could fly along at 8,000 or 10,000 feet, and they would be ranging you and they could fire a burst . . . which could bracket you.

I was doing a photographic flight one day, in cloud, probably about 8,000 or 10,000 feet, and I actually heard the bursts going off around me. I'd been flying too straight and level for just too long, maybe a minute, two minutes, and the predictor guns had focused in and they fired their salvo and there was a burst of four or five or six very bright bursts around the aircraft. Fortunately, not one single thing hit, which was extraordinary because normally when you hear the flak it's very dangerous. But I left that area very quickly.

The Americans had landed in a salient in Normandy. They were around an airfield called Crepeville that used to be a 190 base. We were escorting American bombers down to St Malo, it was just the squadron and . . . probably about fifteen bombers at 12,000 feet . . . I had a section on the starboard side and I crossed over to the other side for the return journey.

I was hit by flak . . . and my engine was hit. It stuttered on for a while, but after a few minutes I realised it was going to pack up . . . I was at about 12,000 feet and I was able to glide and then had to put my flaps and wheels down to reassure the Germans that I was actually in trouble. And that was one of the astonishing things of the war, for me anyway, that I flew over German gun emplacements . . . and did a forced landing at Crepeville . . . and the Germans didn't fire at me.

I stayed at that station for two days . . . they fixed my aircraft up and I flew back to England two days later, but you had to be very,

Left: Vengeance weapon – a V1 flying-bomb, nicknamed doodlebug, just after launch from a site in mainland Europe. Most of the V1s launched at Britain were shot down or fell in uninhabited areas, but, with the V2 rockets, they caused over 6,000 civilian and nearly 3,000 military deaths in the UK in a period of ten months. A further 50,000 were injured. Casualties in the D-Day landing were lighter.

Bottom: 'They equipped us with Tempests.' Before the arrival of the Meteor jet fighter, the Hawker Tempest was the only machine capable of matching the speed of the V1s. The supply of the Tempests to the RAF was delayed by a strike in the factories where they were being built. The machine illustrated is a Mark V which does not yet have squadron markings.

very careful [taking off] because the Americans had warned that the Germans often fired at you when you were taking off or landing. But I considered that they were very good to me that particular day.

Flight-Lieutenant Bill Pauley

Bill Pauley was one of the first pilots over the Normandy beaches on D-Day as part of a recce patrol. Some time earlier, he had escorted bombers attacking what he later learned were assembly plants and launching-pads for what became the greatest threat to London of the entire war: the V1 flying-bombs, or doodlebugs. Just one week after the invasion, the first doodlebugs were fired at London. Flight-Lieutenant Pauley's squadron was then re-equipped with aircraft capable of intercepting these flying bombs, containing up to a ton of high explosive:

There were three lines of defence . . . the guns along the coast, predicted guns, and they ranged in and fired automatically. Then there were fighters, a few squadrons, just behind that, and then behind that around London there was the line of armoured balloons . . . [with] explosives attached to the cables. Our job was to operate between the guns and the armoured balloons. Five-o-one had Spitfires, but Spitfires couldn't catch the flying-bombs. They went normally 400 plus, and the only aircraft that was capable of doing that at ground-level, say at 1,000 feet, was the Tempest . . . at 1,000 feet the Tempest could do about four-twenty, even with long-range tanks.

They equipped us with Tempests and we had to patrol normally at 4,000 or 5,000 feet. They would warn you that flying-bombs, a wave of them, were coming in and you would see them too and then the whole idea was to get above them and behind, not too far behind. Normally, they were going a little faster than the Tempest, but not always, and you used your height to gain speed in the dive, and you would get in, fire at from about 250 yards down to about 150, and then break away and stay inside your patrol area and hope that you had hit it. Normally, you did some damage to it; sometimes it blew up and sometimes it just went down.

Flight-Lieutenant Bill Pauley

Eager to shoot the doodlebugs out of the sky, Tempest pilots would dive at their targets at speeds reaching 500 miles per hour, which left little margin for error. A Tempest could almost be blown out of the sky by too close an approach:

> I was diving down, possibly going faster, quite a bit faster than that particular flying-bomb, and I started firing and realised that I was closing in very, very fast, took a last burst at it and pulled away to my right. But as I pulled away I passed more or less over it and it exploded so that the full force of the explosion actually caught my left wing and punctured it, oh, scores of places, punched holes right through it. It had the effect of spinning the aircraft laterally . . . at night you rely on your instruments to tell you where you are, what position you're in, and when things settled down the aircraft was flying nice and steadily for those few seconds, but I found that the searchlights that they had right round London, warning you of the position of the armoured balloons, they were coming from above rather than from below. I was able to work out eventually that I was upside down and not the right way up.
>
> I got that fixed up and then headed back to base, which was Bradwell Bay. It was fairly straightforward then, but flying was difficult because the perforated wing made it very left-wing heavy. It was very difficult to keep that up and come in and do a left-hand circuit because the whole object is not to let the left wing drop, because if it drops too much then you would go into a spin, which would be even more awkward.
>
> *Flight-Lieutenant Bill Pauley*

The Tempest pilots' role was difficult and dangerous and V1s were not the only danger they faced. Bill Pauley lost one of his friends through engine failure on a patrol:

> My number two was a man called Faraday. One particular night we were up . . . he crashed. He said his engine had cut, and [I] and the ground control told him to check his petrol-tank and check various things . . . but he went into the ground . . . they told him to bale out and he didn't bale out. He had plenty of height. Something happened, he just didn't bale out because his harness wasn't even unlocked.
>
> His sister came across to the funeral. The service was in a chapel quite close to RAF Bradwell Bay, and his sister told me that was the fourth brother, they came from southern Ireland . . . she had lost during the war. I thought that was absolutely remarkable and it just shows the number of people who joined up from southern Ireland. And that Paddy Faraday was the fourth member of her family to have

died during the war. It was very, very sad.

In Europe aircraft were vital to the Allied advance, but the Fleet Air Arm's planes were also needed in the Pacific war against Japan. The British Pacific Fleet launched a series of attacks on Japanese-held islands, while the fighter pilots provided protection against enemy aircraft, especially the *kamikazes* who were prepared to kill themselves to destroy Allied ships:

> I landed on one of the fleet's carriers just after it had had a *kamikaze* and we could see it happening . . . this was where British carriers were much better than Americans because they had a very thick armour-plated deck, whereas the Americans had fancy teak decks and everything just went through. With the British carrier they bounced off, mostly, but scattered everything on deck.
>
> It must have been shocking if you were on the deck of any carrier when a *kamikaze* hit. They didn't have much chance. A lot of them were just trainees. They were locked in the cockpit, they couldn't get out and they were dressed up in their fancy robes and told they were going to heaven and all that; 'Away you go, boy.' They couldn't get out.
>
> *Lieutenant George Boyd*

The war in the Far East finally ended in August 1945 after American B-29 bombers dropped atomic bombs on Hiroshima and Nagasaki. George Boyd's aircraft-carrier was anchored in Yokohama Bay when General McArthur accepted the Japanese surrender on board USS *Missouri*. He and his friends looked on at the formal end of a war that had cost over sixty million lives throughout the world, a war in which air power had played a part far greater than had ever been dreamed of by the men who flew those first flimsy aircraft in the skies over the Western Front in the First World War.

Eyes Over the Ocean

Of all of Germany's weapons, the one that came closest to winning the war was the submarine, or U-boat. German submarines took such a toll of Allied shipping in the Atlantic that, as late as the summer of 1943, the outcome of the Battle of the Atlantic was still in the balance. In March 1943, U-boats achieved their highest-ever monthly tonnage of Allied ships sunk.

Among the resources deployed to combat the German submarine fleet were a number of Consolidated B-24 Liberator long-range bombers of RAF Coastal Command. The Liberator became the scourge of the U-boats, with an Ulsterman the top-scoring 'Ace' of Coastal Command.

Squadron-Leader Terence Malcolm Bulloch thwarted German plans to destroy convoy HX217 as it crossed the Atlantic from Nova Scotia in December 1942. Flying from Iceland, which allowed the mid-Atlantic Gap to be bridged, Bulloch spotted a U-boat on the surface through a hailstorm and dropped six depth-charges on the submerging U-254; it was the end for the submarine.

Little over an hour later Bulloch spotted two more U-boats. One crash-dived, but Bulloch dropped his last two depth-charges on the second. As he continued his patrol over the convoy, the Lisburn man forced another five U-boats to crash-dive, and the plane which relieved him did likewise. Submerged submarines were so slow that the menace to the convoy was eliminated.

Almost singlehandedly Bulloch had seen off a wolf-pack intended to destroy the convoy; HX217 reached the UK with the loss of only one ship. Bulloch's 120 Squadron, based variously at Aldergrove, Ballykelly and in Iceland, was Coastal Command's most successful squadron in the U-boat war, and Terence Bulloch, known as Hawkeye, sank more German submarines than did many squadrons.

U-boat killer Terry Bulloch, the RAF's leading anti-U-boat ace. Here he poses in front of his Liberator.

9
Prisoners of War

After about a week I slept in the morgue every night.

ETWEEN 1939 and 1945 tens of thousands of Allied servicemen
became prisoners of war (PoWs) in every theatre of war. Many
died in captivity, but many more survived to tell the story of life
as a PoW. This chapter includes the stories of two survivors who recalled
their days as prisoners of the Germans and the Japanese.

Squadron-Leader Doug Cooper was flying a Blenheim bomber on a
mission against the Keil Canal in July 1941. Attacking a bridge over the
canal from a height of 600 feet, his plane was hit by anti-aircraft fire and
he and his crew were forced to bale out. Wounded in the ankle, he received
first-aid treatment from the AA gunners who had shot him down and was
then transferred to a hospital in Hamburg, from where he went to a PoW
Camp. Until the end of the war he was a prisoner in five different camps
in Germany and Poland.

Doug Cooper found a variety of attitudes to imprisonment among his
fellow inmates:

> Some people spent as much time as possible in their bunks . . . one
> chappie who spent four years in Germany reckoned that he was only
> conscious for about a quarter of that time. The rest of the time he
> was sleeping; he'd brought sleeping down to a fine art. Others spent
> their time trying to get out, and I was one of those for the first
> three years. And yet others spent the time improving themselves
> by studying.
>
> The warders were ordered to shoot anybody climbing the wire. They
> had no hesitation in shooting anybody climbing the wire, whether they
> were in their sound senses or not. Some people did climb the wire, they

138

went round the bend, and got shot in the process. I knew one man, Ken Toft, from the west of Ireland, who actually crawled out between the wires beneath one of the sentry boxes. [He] got outside the wire but didn't get home, unfortunately.

Most prison-camps had their escape committee, and plans for escape . . . had to be subject to vetting by this committee to make sure various plans didn't clash with each other. This was really brought to a fine art towards the end. [In] one camp . . . we had a tunnel dug . . . which really hasn't been talked about since the war. Up to the time of the Great Escape, which was about a couple of years later, it must have been the longest tunnel ever dug in Germany. It was over a hundred-yards long, it got outside the wire; it was discovered twice by the Germans, a rather ingenious tunnel . . . three men got out through the end of the tunnel but didn't get out of Germany, unfortunately.

There was a mock tunnel. We started off with a ten-foot deep bellows-shaped chamber, from which ran a short twenty-five-foot length of tunnel and, three feet back from the end of that twenty-five-foot tunnel, another short vertical shaft was dropped; the main tunnel started out from that. So, when the Germans eventually discovered the first twenty-five foot, they thought we were crazy to even try digging a tunnel with the wire a hundred yards away; they filled in the first twenty-five feet and called it a day at that. In actual fact, the main tunnel was out beyond the wire by that time, so we got back into the main tunnel again. We had electric light right up to the face, we had a trolley pulling the soil back, and the soil was dispersed underneath the hut and up on the roof.

The hut we were in was known as the workshop. There was hammering and banging and sawing going on all day and every day. The Germans knew this, but what they didn't know was that a tunnel started from there. There was one other crisis, an occasion when we ran out of wire to take the light up to the tunnel face. The Germans in this particular camp, it must have been a mile right around the perimeter, had a tannoy system mounted on telegraph poles strung round the camp. One evening at dusk, we had a team of boys at the foot of each pole who, at a given moment, shinned up the poles, cut the wire down and it was all bundled down our tunnel. So [the] next morning the Germans had no tannoy system and didn't know where the devil the wire had got to.

I was in Stalag Luft Three. There were four different compounds there, and the Great Escape took place in the north compound. I was in the east compound, that was the one where the 'Wooden Horse' escape took place. But we certainly felt the reaction as a result of the Great Escape . . . fifty men were shot. It cast a real air of gloom, not only on the British PoWs but also on the German Luftwaffe guards. I think they were ashamed of themselves.

They'd escaped, you see, and made their individual attempts to get away and were picked up individually, but, I understand, the orders went out from Hitler and company that they were to be shot. And that's what happened to them. All shot, of course, 'while attempting to escape', that's the way it was put. In actual fact, it was murder.

. . . there was one priceless occasion when a . . . German general made the mistake of actually driving into the prison compound in his open Mercedes . . . and left his driver in charge while he inspected the camp. Well, of course, the job was to try and distract the driver, and the lads got a lot of old papers together, put a match to them, lots of smoke coming out of one of the huts, and shouts of 'Fire, fire!' Eventually this guy's curiosity overcame him and he got out of his car to see what all the noise was about, and within seconds that car was stripped of everything it possessed: maps, documents, the lot. And, of course, there was hell to pay about this and all sorts of dire consequences were threatened unless the items were returned. In actual fact, they were returned within about an hour and in that time every map had been copied, and every article returned, every bit of paper, had been stamped with a stamp: 'Censored by Churchill'.

We let the Germans realise that three people were missing. We kept them covered up for about three days. By then the Germans had discovered there were three missing, but they didn't know who the three were. So they had a roll-call and identity check. It was a very slow operation and by lunch-time half the prisoners had been checked and sent to the far side of the parade-ground.

So there was a big mob of lads [at] each end of the parade-ground, one lot checked, one unchecked. And by common consent the two crowds made a bee-line for each other and mingled up the middle of the parade-ground, and the Germans had to start again from scratch. They were very cross about that. They ordered another parade about an hour later, after lunch, and the Senior [British] Officer said, 'No, we're not going on parade again.' He gave us orders to stay inside the huts, which we did, and the Germans came along with tin-hats, tommy-guns, the lot, and [put] a burst of fire into every hut, and you never saw us get out on the parade-ground so fast in your life.

We marched east in the winter of 1944-45 to a camp in Hamburg. When we got there, there was literally nothing at all. We were shown into rooms with just a bare concrete floor and straw . . . that was about the lowest state we ever reached. We really didn't have to stay there too long, thank God, because the war was near the end . . . we marched out of there towards Lübeck and [by] that stage the guards were a pretty elderly bunch, so much so, actually, [that] we were carrying the rifles for them.

We never did get to Lübeck. We were told a typhus epidemic had broken out there and the senior German officer said, 'Find yourselves billets somewhere and wait to be released.' So we found a rather nice spot, a little village around a lakeside, settled ourselves down there and waited for Montgomery's boys to come and bring us home.

The last few weeks we were living the life of Riley, really. We went out foraging food around the farms, the weather was perfect and we came home brown as berries and as fit as fiddles.

Doug Cooper had been a PoW for five months when Japan entered the war. The speed of the Japanese advance surprised the Europeans and Americans, and by early February 1942 the Japanese army had captured Malaya and was attacking the major British naval base of Singapore. On 15 February the officer commanding Singapore, Lieutenant General Percival, surrendered to the Japanese. His action was a shock to the men under his command, who thought that they were going to fight on in the hope that part of the garrison at least could be evacuated. Their shock was not lessened by the knowledge that they were going to become prisoners of the Japanese, for they already knew of the reputation of the Imperial Japanese Army in China.

On that day some 80,000 British, Australian, Indian and Malay servicemen entered captivity in the greatest single defeat ever inflicted on a British army. Among those prisoners was **Sergeant Eric White** of the Royal Corps of Signals, who had served in Malaya since 1938. He was to serve time in a total of thirteen different camps. In the first of these, at Kamburai, life was at least bearable; however, this was soon to change. The next camp he went to, Konyu Two, which was about a hundred miles away, was a labour camp for the infamous bridge over the River Kwai:

> Then we started work at the railway and, of course, it was then the trouble started. There were beatings every morning, there were beatings every night, and the hospital would be turned out. They just wanted so many men, I've seen them carried out on stretchers to work.
>
> They were boring holes in the rock and that was piece-work too, so a fella on a stretcher could hold the tool that you drill in and another fit fella would hit it. I had a short session on that when I got sick. But most of the time I was with the elephant boys, and that was the luck of the draw, although you still had the same tasks to do. Our Japs didn't seem to be as bad, anyway, as some of the ones on the actual railway itself. It was just their system to try and get more work out of you. That was it, full stop. They had a quota of work to do and that was their system . . .
>
> In the wet weather it was bloody awful, slipping and sliding. I only did a month and that was when I was sick. I completely passed out. I don't know what happened to me . . . but I came to in a makeshift place where there were fellas sleeping . . . and there was this Australian medical officer . . . feeding me this soup thing with some blood in it and he was just feeding me like a baby. I don't know what happened to me . . . it was probably just sheer, absolute exhaustion. People were dying pretty rapidly by this time . . . .
>
> When you were sick, one of the things you had to do was to dig a grave, and of course you never knew if you were going to go into the bloody thing or not. Anyway, they started to evacuate [the] sick. That sounds great, but they only evacuated down people who they thought would recover. It was only a Jap sergeant or somebody [who] would have a look at you and say, 'You go' or 'You don't', rather like the Germans and the gas chambers . . . . [It] was the same with us, and what our people used to do was to try to pick an NCO or two who looked like death warmed up but, at the same time, wasn't all that bad and he went in charge of them. So I went off with a party of twenty-five with no guards.
>
> They just told you to walk to the next camp and away you went. You got rice when you left but you got nothing else; if you had a water-bottle you got water. We hid stretchers out in the jungle so that [we could

carry] some of the lads who wouldn't make it . . . before we got to the other end, we had to dump the stretchers, or if you met a Jap you had to dump the stretchers. Anyway, we got to the other end, to Konyu One, which was the base camp . . . and it was a bad place.

They were all permanent huts and they were absolutely walking with bugs and lice and things like that and everyone was really depressed and dejected. I couldn't sleep in the huts at all, and they wouldn't let you sleep outside. It was fine weather by this time, so I slept in the morgue; after about a week I slept in the morgue every night . . . there were bodies in it but there were no bugs, lice or anything there, you see. I had to be up early and out and away back down but I wasn't far from where the latrines were so I could always say that's where I went.

We got onto barges and we got down, then, to Tarso. The food wasn't bad in Tarso. There weren't many active workers there. The railway had already arrived . . . and anyone who was fit had gone on, but the [Kempeitei – Japanese Gestapo] headquarters was there and that was a bad place to be, and there was a lot of brutality there. However, anyway, it was there that I got renal colic, and our officer nearly had a bloody fit . . . because he thought I had cholera, for there was cholera around. But this was the sort of camp, too, that when you slept at night a lot of the lads had these big tropical sores and they put rice poultices on [them]. There was no shortage of rice in this particular camp and there [were] reasonably good, by our standards anyway, vegetables, but the meat and stuff was non-existent. But the rats would come and try to eat the rice. I had one pull a lot of hairs out of my head, you'd think he was trying to make a bloody nest. This was the sick bay.

Well, I got over the renal colic. I was carried up past the [Kempeitei] place feet first, and they did give me a salute, but I said to myself, 'You so-and-sos'.

There was this bridge called Wan-Po. It wasn't really a bridge, it was a cutting that was cut into solid rock . . . snaking along the edge of the cliff [bottom] . . . that was a bad place to be, too. However, anyway, by this time I'd gone back up country and it was then we went away off across, nearly to [Tavoy], walking and carrying stores, walking and carrying stores, walking and carrying stores.

By this time [our] bombers were coming over and the day before they'd taken the bridge down, the viaduct bridge . . . we were shifting stores from the barges up to the railway to go on up country . . . I don't know how the fellas were living up there because there wasn't much going up. Anyway, the next thing this train pulled in, and out of the wagons got these wounded and they came to us for water. You nearly always had water, because the Japs themselves wanted water, boiled water. And the Japs went bloody mad when the wounded ones came over, knocked hell out of us and lined us all up and told us off in Japanese.

I don't know what the hell they said, but we got the gist of it anyway, and they would not give their own wounded water and they beat us for doing it, especially the NCOs . . . they were still coming out of the wagons and the last two to come out of [the] wagons were two fellows who had no legs. They were all swollen up with beri-beri and gangrene, you could smell it a bloody mile away. Well, our lads broke ranks and carried them down to the barges, and the Japs couldn't understand it at all, because, you see, in the Jap army if you were wounded you'd get no pay and half-rations.

We did get paid while we were working. It worked out at the price of an egg a day, roughly speaking, and if you were in charge of a party you got a little bit more pay, but anyone who was sick got no pay and the ration calculation for him was only half of what the working man got. As far as we were concerned, everyone divided it out evenly, and the money, well, there was always money deducted off whatever you got . . . [by] the corrupt Japs.

We went to this place, and the lads who were working were . . . digging tunnels into the hills, presumably for a last stand, I don't think it was mining or anything like that. But I got lucky, got a job in the cookhouse, and there was a lance-corporal from the Northumberlands who was in charge, and I just did what he told me and was quite happy to do so. And the food was good by now.

I probably hold the record for being the last man to be beaten up in that camp. By this time they were roll-calling maybe two or three times a night; you had your roll-call every morning and every night. They were very strict about it . . . and at night there were two of our people did guard on the huts, one at each end. If you went out to spend a penny, which you would do quite often, then you took a [bamboo] stick out of one pot and put it in the other and the British guard kept count.

Then the Japs came along . . . and counted the number of sticks in one pot and the number in the other and then counted the number of people. The British fella had a note of how many were there but [the Japanese] had one as well, so there was a count taken of how many were at the loo. They never came to the loos to [check]. On your bedspace you had a tally with your Japanese number on it . . . and you had the same tally on your waist. So, if they wanted to check up who you were and what you were they just read this thing off and they would sometimes search your kit when you weren't there. If they found anything that shouldn't be there then you were [beaten].

When you went out you turned the tally up and when you came back you put it down, and I forgot to put the bloody thing down. This Jap woke me up. Well, he created holy stink, a torch in your face and bash, crash, he went on his way. The next night I was woken up again and I thought, 'God, I'm for it', but it wasn't [the Japanese]. It was one of our lads saying that the word had come back that the Japs were about to surrender, or had surrendered, but 'don't let on you know, try and keep discipline'.

The Japs were getting very jumpy. One day we were arguing like hell amongst one another whether the war was over, or whether it wasn't. The Siamese were all outside telling us it was over, but we daren't move. The next thing, in comes the Jap dispatch-rider. There were about 5,000 in the camp, so there were 10,000 eyes glued on this fella, and he handed over the roll of messages, and the Jap commandant read up and down, up and down, up and down. His face got longer – if a round Jap face can get long – but you know what I mean, and he dashed back in.

There were two of them, the sergeant and himself, and they left their swords and kept their revolvers and then they had an argument and went back and left their revolvers and put their swords back on. They were monkeying around like this while we were all watching, but they came to the office, which was quite near the hut I was in, and Sergeant-Major Simpson came out and it was just as if he was on parade. He had his medals, his Sam Browne, the only thing he hadn't got was his sword and, of course, this took the wind out of the Japs' sails straight away to see him all dressed up like that.

But then out came our bugler. Now, the bugler we had blew the Jap call, but this time he came out . . . and called general assembly. Well, there were fellas who were sick and and hadn't moved; they were off their beds. It was an amazing sight.

That was August 1945 and on that parade ground, as a Union Flag was run up, prisoners cheered, cried, prayed and looked forward to going home. Aircraft dropped medical officers and supplies as well as food and clothing, and gradually the survivors were prepared for the journey home. Eric White went to Rangoon for a medical examination to see if he was fit enough to travel home, or if he would have to go to India to convalesce. At the end of his time in captivity he weighed only six-and-a-half stone.

Yet he was one of the lucky ones, for thousands of his comrades died in the labour camps along the Burma railway and in the copper and coal mines of Formosa and Japan itself. The Japanese soldier had been a cruel opponent and a cruel captor, and many of the cruelties inflicted on the prisoners have not been mentioned. Of all the men who celebrated the return of peace in that summer of 1945, few could have done so with as much enthusiasm as those who had been PoWs.

After Tobruk

Squadron-Leader Doug Cooper and **Sergeant Eric White** survived the PoW camps, but many others died, some from starvation or ill-treatment, others while trying to escape or, tragically, through the actions of their own forces.

In June 1942 all but a few men of 5 Light Anti-Aircraft Battery, from North Down, were captured when Tobruk fell to Rommel. Most were imprisoned in Italy and many tried to escape. **John Atcheson** and **Jim Pritchard** succeeded, Atcheson living for a time with an Italian family before he was betrayed by Fascists. Pritchard was recaptured after three months of freedom and remained a PoW until Allied troops liberated his camp.

John Atcheson was among many PoWs who were sent to Germany by train. Near Florence the train was attacked by Allied bombers and about 700 men were killed. Atcheson escaped, but was again recaptured and spent the rest of the war as a PoW. Two other members of 5 Light Anti-Aircraft Battery, **Tom McCutcheon** and **Willie McBlain**, died in captivity, McBlain in an attack by RAF aircraft.

Eric White in happier days before the fall of Singapore. His pet ape went into captivity with him.

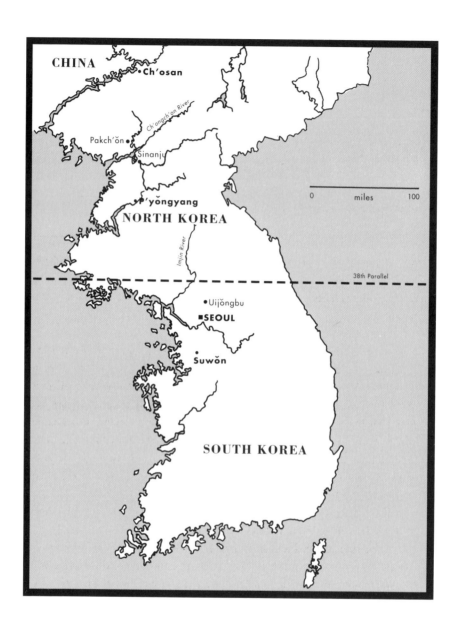

10
Korea

All of a sudden a grenade came into the river.

THE KOREAN WAR began in June 1950; in November 1st Royal Ulster Rifles arrived in Pusan as part of 29 Infantry Brigade. They had a rapid introduction to war as they travelled northwards by train to the main war zone.

> We got to about halfway up Korea . . . and apparently there were about five trains all lined up outside this tunnel, because the enemy were [believed to be] in this tunnel. So, whoever it was decided that the Royal Ulster Rifles would go through . . . first. It was very creepy, a great big, long tunnel, and we were all thinking we were going to be blown up and the enemy [were] going to ambush us in this tunnel. I remember driving through this in the train with the rifles facing out, and we got through the tunnel and met nobody at all and then all the other trains followed up behind us.
>
> Eventually we got to a base . . . and were sent off to a place called Uijongbu and at Uijongbu I was sent off, the first time I'd ever really got on a fighting patrol. I was in charge of about half of B Company and we went on a sweeping patrol. This was about a hundred miles behind the lines, but there were [thought] to be enemy guerrillas in these hills. We went off down the road, I remember the sergeant-major and myself in the middle and three platoons out in front, and we suddenly met about 250 guerrillas.
>
> These were bandits who were . . . behind the front line who really wanted to surrender . . . they surrendered to me and that was quite exciting. We lined them all up and marched them back to battalion headquarters where the commanding officer couldn't believe it, that

149

we had captured all these people. Anyhow, that was the story of my first patrol.

Captain Robin Charley, B Company

In the weeks that followed the battalion experienced a side of Korea they had not expected. They had thought of Korea as a hot eastern country; as winter approached, however, the men found conditions far from tropical.

At night, once you touched metal with your hands, your bare hands, you left the skin on the metal. You used to stand on sentry, you always had a couple of sandbags, filled them with straw, stuck the feet in, and that's what kept you going.

Company Sergeant-Major Sean Fitzsimons

Just before the battle of Happy Valley we got fresh rations, a couple of slices of bread, two frozen oranges and two bottles of beer. The bottles were lager-sized bottles and we had the short bayonets then that didn't reach down to the bottom and, as you could guess, with that cold there was just about an inch of alcohol at the bottom of the bottle and the rest was just frozen beer . . . or water. So it was smash the bottle, hoke the ice out and have a wee drink at the raw alcohol and throw the orange at somebody and hit him with it; it was no use, no way were you going to eat it.

Corporal Joe Lavery

You had, supposedly, 'oil low-cold test' that was Arctic-tested to keep any moving part moving, no matter how cold it was. That even froze, with the result [that] you were sitting at night, especially on a machine-gun, and you just had to keep moving [the working parts] back and forward all night to keep them free, just in case they were needed.

Company Sergeant-Major Sean Fitzsimons

We thought it was great lighting a fire, and then once you put the sole of your boot up to the fire the sole just fell off. It would make you cry, especially at a place called Uijongbu. The wind just blew straight down that valley and it was terrible. And then the other thing

Korea. A soldier of the Royal Ulster Rifles, wrapped up against the cold, looks out over a frozen landscape of hills and paddyfields.

too, having to live in the slit-trenches, because that's all we had, we never got into any buildings.

Sergeant Nat Kennedy

Nobody ever thought what the weather would be like or what it wouldn't be like. It was . . . a lazy wind; it would go through you, it wouldn't go round you. And your breath, it was snow coming out . . . but people [were] never prepared for it and by the time they got prepared for it the bloody war was over.

Major Tom Smith, Quartermaster

This lack of knowledge about the climate in Korea was exemplified by the tropical kits supplied to British soldiers in Korea. Tom Smith earned the respect of everyone in the Rifles for his efforts to ensure that his troops were adequately provided with clothing to combat the Korean winter. After moving almost up to the Chinese border, UN forces had to retreat in December 1950 after a massive counter-attack by the Chinese and North Koreans. They withdrew to the area of Seoul where, in January 1951, the Rifles had their first major action in another vicious attack by their enemy:

On 1 January 1951, we were in positions just north of Seoul at a place called Happy Valley. We took up positions about midnight, and then at about 4.00 in the morning one of our platoons was approached by some people up the side of a hill saying, 'South Koreans, we surrender.' And the boys stood up out of their slit-trenches and then got rushed and these were actually Chinamen, they weren't South Koreans at all, it was a ruse.

We then organised a counter-attack against this position on top of the hill. One of our officers, called Ivor Daniel, who was platoon commander of the reserve platoon of B Company, was ordered by the company commander to do a counter-attack and it was . . . just as we'd learned at the School of Infantry. He said, 'Fire Section there, numbers 2 and 3 Sections, follow me', and he did a right-flanking, charged the enemy with covering fire from the Fire Section and Bren guns and it worked exactly as per the book. I was there standing watching it with the sergeant-major. I remember we were thinking how well it was all done, and they suffered no casualties at all. They drove the Chinese off the top of the hill and we reoccupied Hill 195.

Captain Robin Charley

The Chinese soldier was good. Once he came at you . . . there was no stopping him. He came in [such] big numbers too that you'd find a crowd coming at you, the first man would have a weapon, three or four behind him would be only carrying ammunition for that weapon. Once the man with the weapon fell, another bloke just took it up and . . . came on.

Company Sergeant-Major Sean Fitzsimons

You've heard the expression 'cannon-fodder'. That's all they were. You could never beat them, they'd just keep on coming. You could shoot hundreds and hundreds, but there were still more coming behind them and you hadn't got enough ammunition to keep up to it.

Sergeant Nat Kennedy

Inevitably, there were casualties.

I was taken prisoner with tops of boots and heels and no soles and I spent about two months marching through freezing cold. Where other people could sit down and have a rest, I had to keep moving about because I'd end up with frostbite. You can imagine [that] with inadequate clothing and probably at the most a tiny little bowl of rice gruel or corn, millet, sorghum or beans about twice a day – [which] wasn't enough as a warmer-up for a meal, never mind a meal to keep you going and keep out cold conditions like that – people very quickly lost weight and started to . . . die of starvation.

I went blind for about three or four weeks. I found out later on it was through malnutrition, but luckily enough that came as the summer was [approaching] and everybody was out, pulling all sorts of plants and leaves and boiling them up, and that, I think, was the thing that saved my eyesight because I started to get at least the greenery out of whatever was growing on the ground.

In one camp we called the Bean Camp, because that's all we lived on, there were about 400 people [within] a month [who] died there, and there were only about fourteen or fifteen of us that walked out of it alive. It wasn't necessarily all starvation. A lot of it was done by our own side's planes coming over, machine-gunning and rocketing us night and day,

Prepare to fire! A mortar-crew are about to open up with their weapons. The two soldiers standing in this photograph are trying to keep warm, one with a leather jerkin, the other with what appears to be American-issue clothing.

because the Chinese were using it as a staging-post. Later on, when we were being debriefed coming out, I mentioned the fact that, 'Surely to goodness, you must have known there were prisoners of war there', and I was told, 'Oh, yes, we did, but the important thing was to stop the staging of the weapons from the Chinese down south.' They said, 'You were a prisoner of war then so you really were expendable.'

I didn't, luckily enough, have anything to do with the North Koreans. Some other people were prisoners of war with them, and they were really vicious and cruel. It was the Chinese that I was under. There's no guarding people who are sitting starving; you didn't really need to do a lot of guarding. If you had escaped, where would you go to with miles and miles and miles of frozen snow and no food and no chance of getting any?

They were treating us as they would treat peasants . . . so I think it was easy to resist the brainwashing, but it was the continuous, non-stop pushing at it, pushing at it, pushing at it [that] started to push their ideas over to some people who were influenced. But I would say there were no NCOs ever turned over to them and the vast majority had too much pride in their own regiment to allow themselves to be turned over to a communist ideology or anything like that.

Corporal Joe Lavery

I was a sergeant in C Company of the Royal Ulster Rifles and we were up on this hill this day, and the company commander asked me to take a patrol down across about two hills away to see if there were any Chinese there. So I got myself [three] men and we got into the valley. I stationed one man on the road, another one halfway up it and took a fella called Pratt and myself, and we were going up to see over the side of the hill.

But before we could do that the chap on the road fired the Verey pistol and that brought machine-gun fire down, and so we had to move forward . . . we got into this river. So we lay in the river and this spotter-plane kept coming up and down. I waved my hat at the spotter-plane and he waved his wings at me. This went on for a good bit, we must have been lying in the river for a couple of hours, and all of a sudden a grenade came into the river. So the both of us dove out of the river up the bank, and there [were] these two Koreans with their rifles pointed and a Chinese officer.

He gave us a signal to turn around. We stood there and I took a deep breath because I thought I was going to be shot in the back. Instead of that your man put his hand on our shoulders and got our ID discs. I think if we had been American they would have shot us. The next thing they took off us was our paybooks, and then he kept pointing thataway there . . . . I said to your man Pratt, 'These guys are going to shoot us.' So we kept on going, we didn't want to run . . . we kept on walking. We got a couple of hundred yards away from them and nothing happened . . . these Korean houses usually had a big hedge around them, about six-foot thick, and I don't know what happened, but me and your man Pratt walked through this hedge and we got to this Korean house.

The old man and a couple of men [were] in it and they gave us a drink of hot water. That was a great thing then, hot water. We later found out that Smith was wounded and crawled back as well, but the chap called Lyons who fired the Verey pistol was [captured] by another patrol of the Chinese and died in a Chinese prisoner-of-war camp.

Sergeant Nat Kennedy

The best-remembered battle of the Korean War was on the Imjin River in April 1951 when a full Chinese army attacked 29 Brigade. It was a bitter and confused battle:

We were just about to move from the reserve position up to relieve the Northumberland Fusiliers, who were actually in the line at that time. But just as we were about to move up to relieve them and let them enjoy a good St George's Day the whole thing blew up. A Chinese army started to come and mess things up and the whole thing just developed into chaos. They just hit us before we could do anything about it, and you had to more or less stand and fight your ground where you were. We managed, along with the Northumberland Fusiliers and a Belgian battalion, to fight our way back and get out of it.

Company Sergeant-Major Sean Fitzsimons

RSM Alex Patterson made his way out from the Imjin on a tank without realising how close he had come to being captured:

When we got the word to withdraw, the Gloucesters had been almost

surrounded. We got the word . . . to make our way up over the hills
and get out the best we could . . . it was more or less every man for
himself. I can remember the getting out all right. The Chinese were
. . . coming over the hills, trying to catch up with us, and they were
coming along the valley to cut us off. They were not more than about
400 or 500 yards from us, and by the time I got down the hill I could
see them within one hundred yards, firing away at us.

But . . . two tanks were firing at the Chinese and I managed to get
onto one . . . and that's how I managed to get out of the Imjin battle.
. . . a couple of years after I got home . . . my brother-in-law went to a
dance in Ballymena and, while at the bar, heard someone mention the
Ulster Rifles. So he says, 'Do you know Alex Patterson of the Ulster
Rifles, an RSM, he's my brother-in-law?' And the chap says, 'Yes, I
remember Alex Patterson alright, because if I had moved down the
last hill when he said, "Let's go!" I wouldn't have been taken prisoner
of war', because he waited for about a minute, taking cover behind the
rocks from [Chinese] fire . . . and when he moved out about a minute
after me, when he got to the bottom of the hill he was taken prisoner,
the Chinese were all around him. So I was lucky, I didn't realise how
close I was to being a prisoner of war.

Those who tried to use the gully route after Alex Patterson were captured
or killed. There was another way out – over the hills – although that was
also dangerous:

I stuck to the hills and it must have been for miles and miles with
the Chinese shouting down from the top of the hills, 'Tommy, this isn't
your war. British Tommy, hand your rifle up, this isn't your war.' But
we just kept plodding on and then we came to where all the firing
was behind us.

I saw this pool of mucky water, I was dying of thirst and I dived into
it and the next thing was . . . Chinese burp-guns opened up into the
pond of water. We got ourselves out, we rolled away from that, [ran]
another few thousand yards until we came to the top of the hill, looked
down and [saw] the withdrawal . . . the American . . . convoys.

We mostly fell down the hill, we'd no power in our legs, threw
ourselves down the hill onto the MSR [main supply route]. I jumped
on the mudguard of an American Red Cross ambulance, and he took

The bridge is down but the work of the engineers allows this jeep-borne patrol of the Rifles to cross the river on a causeway.

us a few miles where the convoy was going. We rendezvoused in this area. We were put: American troops here, Belgian troops there, British on one side . . . from there we were split up again into . . . our own battalions and then we were taken to a place of retirement for two or three days and formed up again.

Corporal Norman Sweetlove

In January at Happy Valley over 200 Rifles had been killed, wounded or captured and those losses were equalled at Imjin. Since the beginning of the year, almost half of the battalion had become casualties:

As far as I can remember we were told that we had lost somewhere between 150 and 200 men. That was when we checked up the next morning and everyone was counted. It must have been nearly 200 missing.

RSM Alex Patterson

But the Chinese advance had been broken at Imjin. The UN Army then counter-attacked, and once again the Ulster Rifles found themselves dug in along the Imjin River where a static war was beginning:

When the battalion moved up again it was just a clean move up to the Imjin itself. The Gloucesters and the Northumberlands were there also. We were static there and we sent patrols periodically over the river . . . but, as far as fighting was concerned, there was no more fighting, only patrols going out.

We had snipers along the river. I was a regimental signaller, my duty was to lay telephone lines. I was told to take a line-party up to a sniper, to lay a line, the sniper being Vimpo Dunwoody . . . . I stopped my line party about a hundred yards off the Imjin and carried the cable the last hundred yards myself, for everything had to be hush-hush.

So I took the last hundred yards myself up to the tree where the sniper, Vimpo Dunwoody, was. When I got to the tree I whispered up the tree, 'Vimpo, I'm here to lay a telephone line, you're to report at night to HQ.' As soon as Vimpo moved his head, 'bang', there was another sniper on the other side spotted that movement from him. Of course, Vimpo fell down the tree and I thought he was shot, but he wasn't shot, lucky enough. So it meant me connecting the phone myself, phoning up HQ and saying to headquarters that Dunwoody had been spotted and that he'd have to get another position. I was told then to bring him back with me to headquarters.

Corporal Norman Sweetlove

After the Imjin the line had [been] consolidated . . . we started to move back up again. The Belgian battalion in our brigade, they moved forward and took the actual positions in which we had that skirmish. The colonel then sent for a representative from each company to go forward once they had cleared the ground, because they had found one or two bodies lying around the place.

So we went up to help identify them and we searched the whole area and got quite a number of our bodies, which had been left where they fell and, fortunately, because of the cold the bodies were intact . . . more or less embalmed . . . we got them together, we buried them temporarily in a mass grave on the spot with due honours and a service and then eventually the Graves Commission came and took each individual body back to Pusan, where they were interred in the United Nations Cemetery.

Company Sergeant-Major Sean Fitzsimons

The Rifles were involved in a number of less serious actions until October 1951 when they left Korea. But they had to wait two years – in Hong Kong – before returning to the UK. Major Tom Smith was there to see them home:

They arrived in Colchester on a Sunday. The town was lined with people from the station to the barracks, roughly two miles away. They were about ten deep to welcome the RUR . . . never done before, never heard of before by any regiment. That was how they were thought of for what they had done before they went out to Korea. There was no trouble, and people used to go along to them and anything they would want they got it from the RUR. But, as I said before, I never had seen or heard of a regiment being so welcome back in the town.

Hearts and Minds

Among the memories of Korea for the Rifles were some that were pleasant. These included memories of friendships, not only with their own comrades but also with the people of South Korea. **Alex Patterson** still communicates with an orphan he befriended during the war:

> [One day] a Korean boy, who was one of the displaced persons at the time just after the Imjin battle . . . came to me and asked could he be my houseboy. I said certainly. While we were sleeping in our slit-trenches at night I used to put him into one of my ammunition-wagons . . . he used to sleep with an army blanket over him to keep [himself] warm.
>
> We used to sit down and he used to say to me, 'You teach me English', and I used to point to different things and say, 'That's a hill' and 'That's a stream' and things like that. That boy today is a professor of economics and he's also the dean of Kyunghee University in Seoul. He wrote to me [when] I came home. [In] the second or third letter he wrote to me he said that he was at college and he loved Byron's poems; could I get him a copy? So I went down to Erskine Mayne's and bought him a book of Byron's poems and I sent it out to him. Cost me a lot of money to post, but it was worth it and he treasures that book to this day.

Conclusion

THE experiences described by the many contributors to this book have covered almost half a century and spanned much of the globe. Campaigns from 1914 to 1951, involving actions from the middle of the Atlantic to the waters of the Far East, have all seen sons of Ulster play a prominent role. In the two world wars of this century it is worth remembering that the service of every Irishman, from whatever part of the island, was given freely; conscription was never introduced to Ireland in the First World War, nor was it extended to Northern Ireland in the Second World War. These stories are, therefore, the stories of men who decided that it was their duty to fight against wrong: the rape of Belgium in 1914 or the scourge of Nazism a quarter century later.

The recent past has seen the end of the Cold War as the Soviet Empire collapsed. Only with these developments has the final chapter of the story of the Second World War been written, as nations which saw Soviet troops replace Germans in 1945 at last said 'good-bye' to their guests. But in a sense, the echoes of the First World War are still with us. I write these lines on the anniversary of the very day in 1914 when Archduke Franz Ferdinand and his wife, the Duchess of Hohenburg, were assassinated in Sarajevo and, almost eighty years later, Sarajevo is again headline news across the world.

As the map of Europe changes, it is almost as if a 1914 map was being recreated. Woodrow Wilson's disastrous planning helped cause the Second World War. As Wilson's remapping exercise is at last consigned to history, we are reminded that knowledge and understanding of the past are essential to a real appreciation of what is happening in our world today. When the Korean crisis occurred in 1950, most people in Europe did not even known where Korea was. The Korean War was a United Nations war, with soldiers of many nationalities fighting under the UN flag. It was the first UN war and, until 1990, many believed it was also the last. UN involvement in Korea came about after the communist North Koreans invaded South Korea and refused to accept UN resolutions demanding withdrawal. Force was then used to meet force.

When Iraq invaded Kuwait in August 1990 there were many parallels with Korea, which became even more obvious when the UN decided to use force to evict the invaders. UN intervention in Korea was made possible only because the Soviets were not attending meetings of the Security Council, where they would certainly have vetoed military action. By late 1990 the changes in Eastern Europe, and the internal problems of the USSR, meant that the Soviets offered no opposition to the American-led UN intervention in the Gulf.

Once again a UN force was assembled and once again it was successful, more rapidly than almost anyone expected. Included in the UN land forces was an Irish regiment, the Queen's Royal Irish Hussars, who were in the van of 1st (UK) Armoured Division's advance. In Korea the Irish Hussars, then 8th King's Royal Irish Hussars, operated in support of the Royal Ulster Rifles. In the Gulf War the ranks of the Irish Hussars included many sons of Ulster, not least their CO, Lieutenant-Colonel Arthur Denaro from County Donegal.

Thus the tangled skein of history contains threads that link the wars remembered in this book as well as the Gulf War of 1991. While the threads that represent the stories of politicians and generals, who by omission or commission brought about those wars – 'Stormin' Norman' has now been added to the litany that includes Montgomery, Patton and many others – are well known, those that represent the experiences of the ordinary man are much rarer.

This book is an attempt to make some small contribution to the story of those ordinary men. The sons of Ulster who have recounted their experiences in these pages deserve to be remembered for their contribution to the history of our century and for the credit they brought to their homeland. And perhaps it is through the stories of ordinary soldiers that the rest of us might finally learn the futility of war.

Bibliography

Barnett, Correlli, *Engage the Enemy More Closely – The Royal Navy in the Second World War* (London: Hodder & Stoughton, 1991).

Bredin, Brigadier A. E. C., *A History of the Irish Soldier* (Belfast: Century Books, 1987).

Denman, Terence, *Ireland's Unknown Soldiers – the 16th (Irish) Division in the Great War* (Dublin: Irish Academic Press, 1992).

Doherty, Richard, *Wall of Steel – the History of 9th (Londonderry) HAA Regiment, RA (SR)* (Limavady: North West Books, 1988).

Falls, Cyril, *History of the Ulster Division* (Belfast: The Linenhall Press, 1922 – reprinted by the Somme Advisory Council, 1991).

Farrar-Hockley, Anthony, *The British Part in the Korean War*, Volume I, *A Distant Obligation* (London: HMSO, 1990).

Foxley-Norris, Sir Christopher (Ed.), *Royal Air Force at War* (London: Ian Allan, 1983).

Gunner, Colin, *Front of the Line – Adventures with the Irish Brigade* (Antrim: Greystone Books, 1991).

Hastings, Max, *The Korean War* (London: Michael Joseph, 1987).

Hastings, Max, *Overlord – D-Day and the Battle for Normandy, 1944* (London: Michael Joseph, 1984).

Hickey, Des and Smith, Gus, *Operation Avalanche – The Salerno Landings, 1943* (London: Heinemann, 1983).

Horsfall, John, *Fling Our Banner to the Wind* (Kineton: The Roundwood Press, 1978).

Horsfall, John, *Say not the Struggle* (Kineton: The Roundwood Press, 1977).

Keegan, John, *The Second World War* (London: Hutchinson, 1989).

Lucas, James, *Experiences of War – The British Soldier* (London: Arms & Armour Press, 1989).

Masters, John, *The Road Past Mandalay* (London: Michael Joseph, 1961).

Mitchell, Gardiner S., *Three Cheers for the Derrys – A History of 10th Royal Inniskilling Fusiliers in the 1914-18 War* (Derry: YES Publications, 1991).

O'Kane, Henry, *O'Kane's Korea* (published privately by author, 1987).

Orr, Philip, *The Road to the Somme* (Belfast: Blackstaff Press, 1987).

Rawlings, J. D. R., *The History of the Royal Air Force* (Middlesex: Temple Press, 1984).

Smith, E. D., *The Battles for Cassino* (London: Ian Allan, 1975).

Trevelyan, Raleigh, *Rome '44 – the Battle for the Eternal City* (London: Secker & Warburg, 1981).

Picture Acknowledgements

Chapter 1

Page 14 Imperial War Museum; *16* Imperial War Museum; *19* Imperial War Museum; *22* Imperial War Museum; *25* Imperial War Museum; *28 (top)* Imperial War Museum; *28 (left)* F. G. T. Robinson.

Chapter 2

Page 36 Imperial War Museum; *41 (top)* Imperial War Museum; *41 (left)* Imperial War Museum; *49* Imperial War Museum.

Chapter 3

Page 54 (top) Imperial War Museum; *54 (bottom)* Richard Doherty; *59* Imperial War Museum.

Chapter 4

Page 69 Imperial War Museum; *72* Imperial War Museum; *75 (top)* Imperial War Museum; *75 (bottom)* Imperial War Museum; *81* Raymond Logue.

Chapter 5

Page 88 Imperial War Museum; *91 (top)* Imperial War Museum; *91 (bottom)* Richard Doherty.

Chapter 6

Page 101 Imperial War Museum; *106* Colonel Harry Porter; *111* Richard Doherty, with thanks to Desmond Whyte.

Chapter 7

Page 113 Richard Doherty; *116* Imperial War Museum; *123* Imperial War Museum.

Chapter 8

Page 127 Hunter McGiffin; *132 (left)* Imperial War Museum; *132 (bottom)* Imperial War Museum; *137* Terence Bulloch.

Chapter 9

Page 147 Eric White.

Chapter 10

Page 151 Royal Ulster Rifles Museum; *154* Royal Ulster Rifles Museum; *158* Royal Ulster Rifles Museum.